Summer Exhibition Illustrated 2014

A Selection from the 246th Summer Exhibition
Edited by Hughie O'Donoghue RA

Summer Exhibition Illustrated 2014

Sponsored by

Insight
INVESTMENT
➤ A BNY MELLON COMPANY℠

Royal Academy of Arts

Contents

Sponsor's Foreword   8

Introduction   10
Hughie O'Donoghue RA

The New RAs: Breaking Down the Barriers   14
Richard Cork

Catalogue

Wohl Central Hall   18
Gallery III   22
Gallery II   40
Gallery I   54
Large Weston Room   64
Small Weston Room   74
Gallery IV   90
Gallery V   104
Gallery VI   118
Gallery VII   136
Gallery VIII   150
Gallery IX   164
Lecture Room   172
Gallery X   186

Index   188
Members of the Royal Academy of Arts   190
Photographic Acknowledgements   192

Sponsor's Foreword

Insight Investment is proud to continue its long association with the Royal Academy of Arts. This is our ninth year as sponsor of the Summer Exhibition, which is celebrating 246 years at the heart of the cultural life of the nation.

Our partnership with the Royal Academy reflects shared values: the importance of excellence, the value of education, a willingness to embrace new ideas and the potency of creative thinking. The Summer Exhibition demonstrates extraordinary diversity; artistic inspiration that mirrors both the vast range and singularity of human experience. It is the world's largest open exhibition and an established part of the summer social calendar.

The partnership between Insight and the Royal Academy is almost as long as the history of our firm. From modest beginnings, a questioning attitude and a willingness to challenge conventional thinking have been the foundations of our approach. Delivering solutions to clients that are suited to their needs has contributed to Insight becoming one of the UK's leading investment managers.

We are honoured that Insight Investment is the lead sponsor of the Summer Exhibition once again in 2014 and we hope that all visitors will be inspired by the skill, passion and creativity on display on the walls and around the galleries.

Abdallah Nauphal
Chief Executive Officer

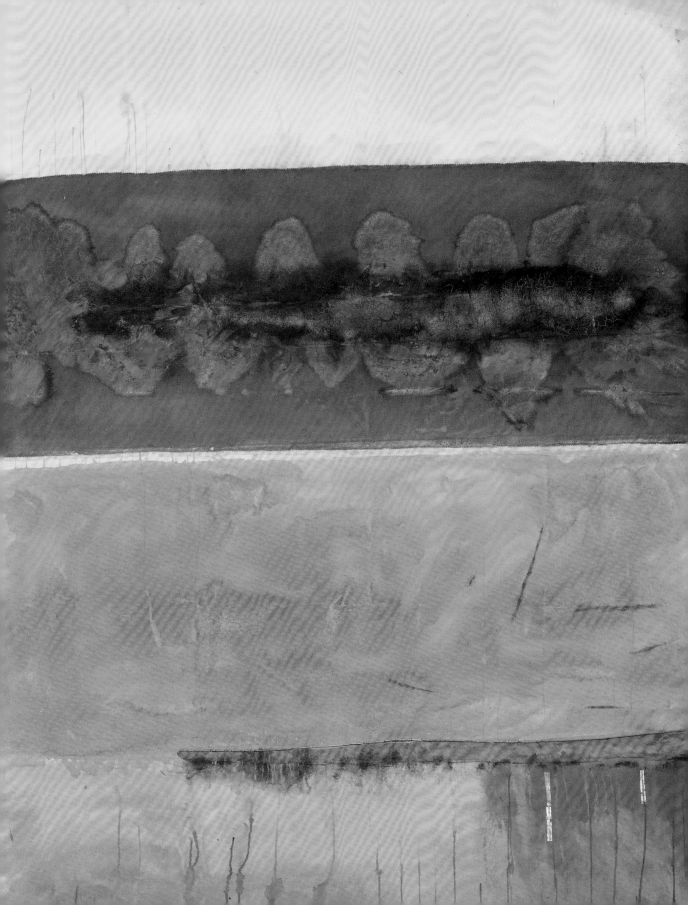

Introduction
Hughie O'Donoghue RA

Remind yourself that all judgements about art are subjective, and that they depend for their validity on the personal, the individual response. They cannot be based on received wisdom.

In 1984 Sir Michael Levy, the then director of the National Gallery, asked me who I thought was the greatest of painters. After I had enthused about a few possible candidates, I said that if I had to choose one, it would be Rembrandt. He said he didn't like Rembrandt. At the time his remark shocked me, but over the years it has often given me pause for thought. It has made me think about the real function of art and how art only really achieves meaning when it is authentically experienced. It's no use anyone else telling you that Rembrandt is a great artist, you have to see and feel his greatness for yourself. You must have the experience. The 246th Summer Exhibition at the Royal Academy is an opportunity to have just such an authentic experience – it is an exhibition unlike any other I know of.

Most of us are familiar with the typical contemporary installation. We may have felt a sense of inadequacy when encountering art luxuriously installed that provokes in us a sense of profound indifference. Whatever our reaction to the art, the space tells us that what we are looking at is important, so we feel any fault must lie therefore with us. The Royal Academy Summer Exhibition is something different: it is a wild garden of strange and exotic passions in which the usual demarcation zones between art practitioners have been swept aside and we are thrown into the uncertain territory of our own judgements. There is of course 'informed opinion'; but wasn't it 'informed opinion' that kept the paintings of Paul Cézanne out of the Paris Salon in the second half of the nineteenth century?

Any institution or academy must seek to renew itself if it is to remain relevant and adequately reflect its time. Recently the Royal Academy has elected an unprecedented number of new Academicians, and their presence is strongly felt at the centre of this year's Summer Exhibition. They are warmly welcomed and celebrated here as evidence of the ongoing vitality of art in the UK. Their work can be seen primarily in the central axis formed by the Wohl Central Hall, extending through the Lecture Room, curated by Cornelia Parker OBE RA, and onwards into Gallery IX.

This year for the first time the open submission was viewed in digital format. Further viewing of the shortlisted works took place in the galleries, and a final selection was made during the hang itself. For me personally, it has been an education looking at the 12,000 or so works submitted. The selectors have tried to be receptive and embrace the process with a generosity of spirit. Nevertheless, I suspect that we may have missed some that should have made it into the exhibition. The subtlety and originality of some works of art can take longer to register than the judging process allows, and if there were omissions of this type I am genuinely sorry.

As exhibition co-ordinator I have seen my role to be that of keeping a view of the exhibition as a whole. However, I have also been solely responsible for the hanging of Galleries III and IV. In Gallery III, the grandest of the Royal Academy's rooms, I have tried to show painting in its purest and most elemental state, a sensory experience of form, colour and material. I did not know what I would have to work with in this room until the very last minute, but what you see was my original idea and I tried to stick with it.

Gallery IV records the transition between painting and sculpture. The hang is anchored by a marvellous sculpture by the late Anthony Caro, which is positioned close to a collaged painting by his lifelong companion, the painter Sheila Girling. Tony had a huge influence on painters as well as sculptors, and the collages, shaped canvases, painted objects and photographs in this room emphasise the increasingly blurred lines that emerged between disciplines in the second half of the twentieth century and continue today.

One hundred years ago, the Summer Exhibition opened with a great sense of order, optimism and permanence. The summer of 1914 has long been remembered as idyllic, an almost Arcadian time of well-being and security. In London the summer season was in full pomp when on 28 June the heir to the Austro-Hungarian Empire, the Archduke Franz Ferdinand, was assassinated in Sarajevo and everything was irrevocably changed. The many legacies of that fateful day are to the forefront of our memory this year as we mark the anniversary of the outbreak of the First World War. In art, the visual irony that first made its appearance in the wake of the great battles fought on the Western Front is still the dominant idiom in contemporary practice.

The other question Sir Michael Levy asked me that day in 1984 was: 'So Hughie, if the National Gallery were on fire and you could take one thing out of it, what would it be?' I resisted the temptation to say 'the fire' and instead chose Titian's *Bacchus and Ariadne*, a voluptuous painting made in the painter's vital years, when he was at the peak of his powers and fame, but also one that reaches back into deep cultural memory to derive its form and meaning. If I could select one painting from this year's Summer Exhibition it would be the wonderfully light *Kranke Kunst*, by Anselm Kiefer HON RA, which seems to float on the wall despite its great size and weight. Evoking comparisons with Claude Monet's groundbreaking *Water Lilies* paintings, it draws our thoughts inevitably to the fields of Northern France.

Overleaf
Anselm Kiefer HON RA
Kranke Kunst (detail)
Mixed media
280 × 380 cm

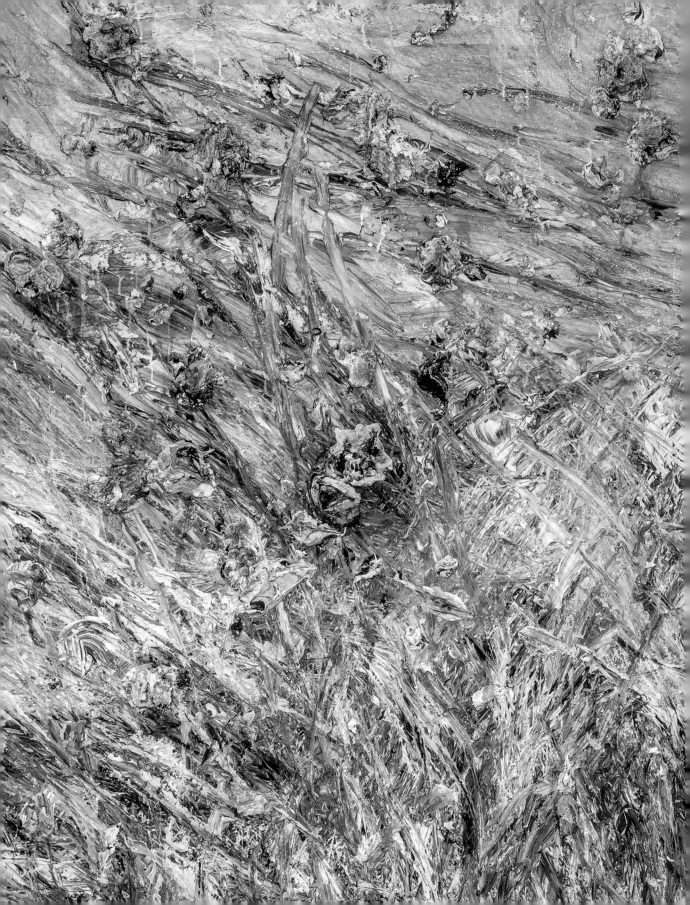

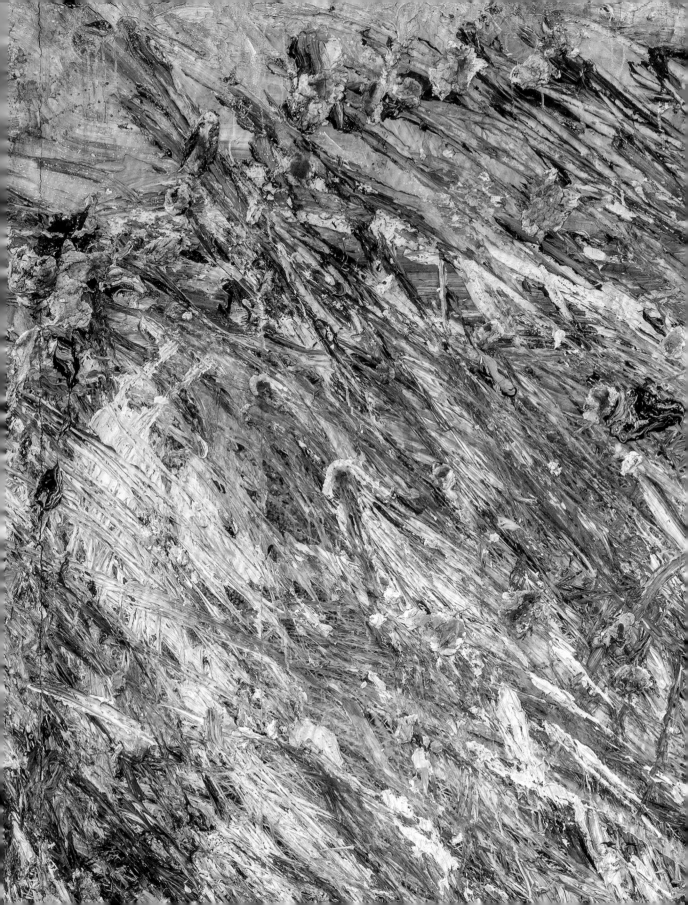

The New RAs
Breaking Down the Barriers
Richard Cork

When Royal Academicians were elected in the past, they usually identified themselves as either painters or sculptors. By the time Lord Leighton became President in the late Victorian period, he had gained a formidable reputation as painter and sculptor alike. But Leighton remained the exception, and only now are the new RAs consistently breaking down all the old barriers, in order to explore fresh, unpredictable ways of working.

Take Thomas Heatherwick CBE, who studied at the Royal College of Art and is described by his mentor, Terence Conran, as 'the Leonardo da Vinci of our times'. He has made public sculpture as explosive as *B of the Bang* outside the City of Manchester Stadium in 2005. But there are no limits to the alternative areas that Heatherwick is also willing to explore. Danny Boyle was so impressed by the eruptive impact of *B of the Bang* that he invited Heatherwick to design the *Olympic Cauldron*, an intensely dramatic highlight of the Summer Olympics and Paralympics in 2012.

Eagerly embracing the opportunity to explore the diverse possibilities offered by architecture, metalwork, furniture design, embroidery and even London buses, Heatherwick abhors 'sliced-up ghettos of thought'. He wants to escape from narrow, blinkered thinking, and showed great aplomb in designing *The Rolling Bridge*, which curls and unfolds across the Grand Union Canal at Paddington Basin. On a far larger scale, the Heatherwick Studio went on to create *Seed Cathedral*, the iconic UK Pavilion at the 2010 Expo at Shanghai. Housing 250,000 plant seeds at the end of 60,000 acrylic rods, the Pavilion became immensely popular and won the Expo's gold medal for design.

Although Conrad Shawcross focuses above all on sculpture, he is equally prepared to experiment and work on immense architectural commissions. Shawcross thrives on a fascination with machines and scientific thought, as well as a consistent interest in philosophical ideas. He has worked in London locations as diverse as the Roundhouse, the Kingsway tram tunnel in Holborn and the Queen's House in Greenwich, where the twelve loops in a work called *Continuum* echoed the geometrical floor originally designed there by Inigo Jones.

By the time Shawcross was invited to make a large, permanent work in Unilever's London headquarters, he could produce an immense *Space Trumpet* and suspend it in the atrium, revolving around a sixty-day cycle more than 23 metres above ground. Then, in an exhibition called 'A Life of Their Own', which I curated at Lismore Castle in Ireland, Shawcross transformed an entire space with a compelling fretwork of lines. They emanated from a cage-like structure in the centre, where a metal engine tipped with a point of light made the cage cast fierce shadows on walls, ceiling and floor.

If Shawcross defies the whole notion of fixed identity, Mike Nelson encourages us to explore labyrinths in which we can easily feel lost. Twice nominated for the Turner Prize, in 2001 and six years later, he constructed an especially nightmarish sequence of claustrophobic interiors at the 2001 Venice Biennale. By transforming a disused brewery on the Giudecca, Nelson invited visitors to negotiate their way through dismal corridors and battered, relentlessly banging doors. Walking on prayer-mats past abandoned sweatshop machinery, we encountered glass doors inscribed 'Sanitary Department Public Entrance'. But at the centre of this labyrinth, which Nelson called *The Deliverance and The Patience*, was a ramshackle bar where model galleons rested on the counter. They revealed his fascination with

William Burroughs's melancholy story of Captain Mission and his doomed utopian colony called Libertatia in seventeenth-century Madagascar.

Nelson was equally uncompromising at the ICA in London, where in 2001 he made an elaborate installation called *Nothing Is True. Everything Is Permitted*. Motivated by a subversive desire to disorientate viewers at every twist of the labyrinth, Nelson succeeded in tantalising, disconcerting and haunting us throughout our complex journey.

His determination to become involved with the darker aspects of human existence is shared by Tim Shaw, a sculptor whose highly provocative art ranges from solitary figures to multimedia environments where light and sound can also play important roles. In one sense, Shaw belongs to an ancient sculptural tradition centred on cast-iron metalwork of monumental proportions, yet he also finds stimulus in exploring an unpredictable array of alternatives. Bent on taking us by surprise, he is not afraid of tackling the most disturbing and macabre subjects.

Since Belfast is his native city, Shaw grew up with gruesome stories of civil unrest and witnessed the results of violent protest. Rather than seeking to escape and concentrate on peaceful, idyllic themes, he places aggression and suffering at the very centre of his art. Nowhere is this more alarmingly apparent than in a 2008 work called *Casting a Dark Democracy*, where the gigantic hooded captive of Abu Ghraib raises both his hands in despair. The materials deployed by Shaw in this work – barbed wire, steel, electric cable and black polythene – are redolent of warfare at its most barbaric.

The most well-known artwork by Yinka Shonibare MBE likewise deals with a battle theme: Nelson's *Ship in a Bottle*, displayed on the Fourth Plinth in Trafalgar Square between 2010 and 2012. Then, after a successful Art Fund campaign, it was purchased for the permanent collection of the National Maritime Museum in Greenwich. This sculpture was, surprisingly, the first Fourth Plinth work to reflect the Battle of Trafalgar, but Shonibare adopted a far from traditional approach to his historical subject.

Born in London, he grew up in Nigeria before returning to study art at Goldsmiths College as part of the YBA generation. Preoccupied with postcolonialism, as well as race and class issues, he has often used flamboyant 'African' fabrics purchased at Brixton market. They made an impact at the Royal Academy's notorious 'Sensation' exhibition in 1997, where Shonibare introduced a trio of headless women dressed in brightly coloured wax-print cotton textiles. Later, in an ambitious 2007 solo show at the new Musée du Quai Branly in Paris, he took as his raw material Fragonard's blithe, manicured paintings of playful seduction. In the doomed *Garden of Love*, Shonibare showed a decapitated aristocratic woman running away from a headless man who offers her a rose.

Although Neil Jeffries usually avoids images of overt violence, he has never been afraid to address personal concerns that other artists might find embarrassing. Fascinated by exploring states of mind, he uses an unconventional combination of oil paint on metal as his preferred medium. A boisterous work like *County Fair* might appear abstract at first glance, but it expresses the energy, confusion and feeling of entanglement that visitors to a fair may well experience.

Jeffries prefers rough-edged, freely handled expression and avoids bland elegance. Trained at St Martin's and the Slade School of Art, he teaches painting and is profoundly involved with medieval art. Yet Jeffries would never advocate an academic approach. On the contrary: he prefers to delve into the fragmented mysteries of everyday life. His London show at Flowers East in 1990 contained works as autobiographical as *Self Study*, in which a trapped figure gazes out of a window at a severed leg isolated on a table. Erotic dreams, angels and duffers filled his early work, and Jeffries continues to be fascinated by frankly incongruous experiences today.

In the past, women were rarely elected as Royal Academicians. Men still predominate to an uncomfortable extent now, but the traditional tide of male supremacy has begun to turn. Even in the architectural profession, where this gender imbalance is very marked, women are now being elected as Academicians more frequently than before. Louisa Hutton is the latest arrival, and over the past twenty years she has gained an international reputation in the Berlin-based practice Sauerbruch Hutton. She founded it in London with Matthias Sauerbruch, who was her fellow student at the Architectural Association. In 1993 they moved it to Berlin, where the practice has achieved a multi-award-winning reputation for major projects.

Outstanding among them is the monumental GSW Headquarters in Berlin, rearing into the sky near Checkpoint Charlie. Colour has always played a vital role in Hutton's work, and when the GSW's window blinds are closed it comes alive with sensuous rose and orange hues. Curving through space, the GSW's double-skin façade is notable for its environmental sustainability. And in 2008 Sauerbruch Hutton used glazed ceramic as a construction material for their shimmering, almost painterly Museum Brandhorst in Munich. Among the many prizes they have won is the Castilla y León International Honour Award for Sustainable Architecture in 2010.

Colour also plays a significant part in Rebecca Warren's sculpture. When she was nominated for the Turner Prize in 2006, several of her works displayed at Tate Britain used acrylic paint, combined with reinforced clay to produce strange, encrusted and provocative apparitions such as *Loulou*. Deliberately lumpy and rough, her sculpture refers back to Degas, Giacometti, Picasso, Rodin and other masters. But there is no hint of deference in Warren's feisty work. She is best known for her uninhibited boldness, creating dramatic figures that look like giant celebrations of oversexed females.

After studying art at Goldsmiths College in London, Warren took an MA in Fine Art at Chelsea College and then gained an artist-in-residence place at the Ruskin School, Oxford, in 1993–94. Her first clay work, *Helmut Crumb*, was made in 1998. It took as its starting point the fashion photographs of Helmut Newton and images by the underground comic artist R. Crumb. Warren was quite open about her sculpture's highly erotic content, declaring that it explored 'territories that are understood as being dodgy'. But Warren also expresses human vulnerability, and reveals a compassionate understanding of the precarious world her figures inhabit. She was recently appointed Professor at the Kunstakademie Düsseldorf.

Chantal Joffe is another artist fascinated by exploring images of women. Yet hers are clothed as well as naked, and Joffe concentrates on portraiture. Born in Vermont, she became a London-based painter after studying at Glasgow School of Art and the Royal College of Art between 1988 and 1994. Her *Self-portrait with Esme*, painted in 2009, shows Joffe almost naked as she bends forwards to hug the smiling child. Although very simplified, this painting shows her interest in family photographs as a source for work, and on one level *Self-portrait with Esme* seems a warm, affectionate

Installation shot of Gallery IX, featuring (left to right):
All Schools Should Be Art Schools by Bob and Roberta Smith RA;
Sieben by Rebecca Warren RA; and *Battenburg* and *Jellyfish in Bristol Channel* by Neil Jeffries RA.

tribute to domestic happiness. But she clutches the child with such strength that the painting also conveys a defensive edge, as if Joffe is determined to protect little Esme from the manifold dangers of contemporary life.

Unafraid of painting on a very large scale, Joffe has even used scaffolding to work on her biggest pictures. She relies on a wide variety of sources, ranging from fashion images and pornography to advertising and the work of the American photographer Diane Arbus. Handling her paint with vigorous freedom, she is driven by a consistent urge to depict women in the modern world. 'I really love painting women,' she told Stella McCartney in a recent interview. 'Their bodies, their clothes – it all interests me.' Her painting *Blonde Girl – Black Dress* won the £25,000 Wollaston Award at the Royal Academy Summer Exhibition in 2006.

Unlike most artists, Patrick Brill operates under a pseudonym: Bob and Roberta Smith. He relishes unpredictability, placing his involvement with writing at the heart of artworks that often use slogans to project their messages. Unlike his father Frederick Brill, who concentrated on landscape painting, Smith also plays music, hosts a radio show and enjoys curating provocative art projects in public spaces. He has produced sculpture made of cement, most notably his controversial *Cement Soup Kitchen* at Beaconsfield Gallery, London, in 2005. But he is perhaps best known for painting brightly coloured slogans, either on strips of wood or banners.

Smith is an instinctive campaigner, whether championing an amnesty on bad art in New York or curating a show called 'Peace Camp' at the Brick Lane Gallery in 2006. Accessibility is important to him, and his 2013 project *The Art Party* supported the idea of artists influencing political thought. Art education is another passion, and Smith is an Associate Professor at the Sir John Cass Department of Art, Media and Design at London Metropolitan University. Yet he leaves the academic world far behind when performing music with his group The Ken Ardley Playboys, or hosting a radio show on Resonance FM called, with disarming directness, *Make Your Own Damn Music*.

Wolfgang Tillmans, by contrast, has always focused on one medium alone: photography. Until now, very few Royal Academicians have shown any interest in the potential of the camera, but Tillmans has been obsessed with photographs ever since his childhood in Germany. He first staged solo exhibitions of his work in Hamburg, but after studying at Bournemouth and Poole College of Art in the early 1990s he decided to base himself in London. The death of his partner, the painter Jochen Klein, came as a tragic loss in 1997. Yet three years later Tillmans's prowess with photographs won him the Turner Prize.

His exhibits in the Turner Prize exhibition roamed freely, from the colossal to the minuscule, and from the panoramic to the intimate. They included anti-heroic images of soldiers but also caught Concorde soaring overhead and, at the other extreme, scrutinised beleaguered passengers on rush-hour Tube journeys. Locations ranged from Hong Kong and Puerto Rico to Las Vegas and New York. In the Royal Academy's 'Apocalypse' show in 2000, Tillmans's exhibits embraced end-of-the-world sunsets and pale still-life compositions as well as erotic intimacy. His appetite for life is voracious and, along with the other newly elected Academicians, he will surely enlarge the Royal Academy's ability to encompass the extraordinary, restless diversity of adventurous art today.

Wohl Central Hall

Over the past year the Royal Academy has elected fifteen new Royal Academicians and Honorary Royal Academicians, the highest number of elections in the institution's recent history. Recognising the importance of these elections both to the Academy and to the Summer Exhibition, the Committee determined to celebrate and draw attention to the work of these artists by exhibiting their work together. This has been done here in the Wohl Central Hall and in Gallery IX, towards the end of the exhibition. These focused groupings suggest that no particular trend can be discerned among those recently elected; the factor common to all is the estimation of their peers.

The works assembled here exemplify this diversity, both in terms of medium and artistic expression. Although they share a common language, the portraits by Chantal Joffe RA and Marlene Dumas HON RA are very different in their focus, with Joffe's figure offering a questioning insight and Dumas's work communicating an emotional state. The intense black square of *Assisted Lines* by Rosemarie Trockel HON RA reveals itself on closer inspection to consist of delicate lines of black wool orchestrated in the manner of a subtle and minimal drawing.

Cake Man by Yinka Shonibare MBE RA comments on the way decadence relies on the labours of others, and suggests that there is a point at which this financial model is no longer sustainable: a tipping point. But there is no tipping point with *Paradigm* by Conrad Shawcross RA, a fine example of his interest in mathematical systems and scientific pioneers. A colossal work by Bob and Roberta Smith RA transcribes a radio interview between the journalist and broadcaster Eddie Mair and the disaster- and conflict-zone surgeon Dr David Nott on the BBC News.

INTERVIEW WITH DAVID NOTT BY EDDIE MAIR 1.1.2014

I WAS A BIT THICK AT SCHOOL AND I HAD TO RESIT MY A LEVELS I WAS DETERMINED I WAS GOING TO BE A DOCTOR. I THINK THE REASON WHY I WAS SO DETERMINED WAS BECAUSE NOBODY THOUGHT I COULD DO IT AND I WAS ABSOLUTELY 100% DETERMINED. MY PARENTS WERE WELL BEHIND ME. SECOND TIME ROUND I GOT INTO ST ANDREWS UNIVERSITY. FROM THAT MOMENT I JUST F L E W EDDIE THAT REALLY INTERESTS ME. I WONDER WHY YOU CONSIDERED YOURSELF THICK OR WHY THE FIRST SET OF EXAMS WAS SO PROBLEMATIC? DAVID. I THINK THEY WERE PROBLEMATIC BECAUSE I DID NOT KNOW HOW TO STUDY. NOBODY SAT DOWN WITH ME. HOW DO YOU STUDY SO HARD TO GET YOUR CORRECT A LEVEL? EDDIE. HOW DID YOU LEARN THAT THEN? DAVID. WELL BECAUSE I FAILED AND I FAILED SO MISERABLY

I WENT HOME AND TOLD MY DAD AND HE SAID NEVER MIND. JUST GIVE THEM ANOTHER GO. AND SO LORD AND THIS TIME I WAS DETERMINED. I WENT TO THE TEACHERS AND I SAID YOU NEED TO TEACH ME HOW TO PASS. THESE EXAMS. THAT WHAT I REALLY NEEDED TO GET TAUGHT. IF YOU DON'T I AM NOT GOING TO BECOME A DOCTOR. AND THE TEACHERS HAD THIS PACT WITH MY PARENTS AND HE SAID HE IS NOT GOING TO GET IN. BUT I WILL JUST GO ALONG WITH IT... I STILL LIE IN BED PINCHING MYSELF. DID I REALLY GO TO MEDICAL SCHOOL? ... IF I MEANT THAT MUCH TO ME. EDDIE. WAS THAT AN AMERICAN YOUNG FROM A VERY YOUNG AGE BECOMING A DOCTOR? DAVID. I WANTED TO BE A PILOT WHEN I WAS A YOUNG BOY MY FATHER WAS AN ORTHOPEDIC SURGEON. HE WAS IN INDIA AND TRAINED IN INDIA. HE WAS ONE OF THOSE TYPICAL INDIAN FATHERS. HE SAID TO ME. YOU ARE NOT GOING TO BE A PILOT YOU ARE GOING TO BE A DOCTOR. IN FACT I DID NOT GET A MULTI LICENCE ... UNIVERSITY I GOT A COMMERCIAL PILOTS LICENCE. EDDIE SOMETHING TO FALL BACK ON IF THE MEDICINE FAILS THROUGH? WELL MORE EXCITING

DAVID. LEARNING TO BECOME A PILOT WAS VERY INTERESTING AND GOING THROUGH ALL THE EMERGENCIES. BUT WHEN YOU ARE ACTUALLY FLYING TO BE HONEST WITH YOU IT'S NOT THAT INTERESTING. BEING A SURGEON IS WHOLLY INTERESTING. EVERY SINGLE TIME YOU OPERATE ON A PATIENT YOU CAN GET YOURSELF INTO TERRIBLE TROUBLE AND REALLY NEED SOME BODY AND EVEN NOW MY HEART IS IN MY MOUTH. MY HEART IS BEATING FAST. THAT PERSON REALLY REQUIRED MY ULTIMATE CONCENTRATION TO GET THROUGH. I THINK MEDICINE. I THINK SURGERY IS A WONDERFUL ART. EDDIE. WHAT DO YOU DO NOW FOR YOUR MAIN DAY JOB? EVERY DAY FOR MOST OF THE YEAR I WORK AT 3 VARIOUS HOSPITALS IN LONDON. I WORK AT ST MARYS WHERE I DO VASCULAR SURGERY AND TRAUMA SURGERY. I WORK AT THE ROYAL MARSDEN WHERE I WORK. WITH THE SARCOMA SPECIALISTS. I HELP THEM TAKE OUT MASSIVE TUMOURS AND HELP THEM DO THE RECONSTRUCTION OF ALL THE BLOOD VESSELS. MY WORK AT CHELSEA & WESTMINSTER WHERE I MAINTAIN MY GENERAL SURGICAL PRACTICE

I DO LAPAROSCOPIC AND UPPER INTESTINAL SURGERY. YOU MIGHT LOOK AT ME AND SAY WHY DO YOU DO SO MUCH? BUT THE REASON IS BECAUSE I WANTED TO KEEP ALL THE PLATES SPINNING. I WANT A GENERAL SURGEON A VASCULAR SURGEON AND A TRAUMA SURGEON. KEEP ALL MY SKILLS UP. EDDIE THAT WOULD BE ENOUGH FOR MOST PEOPLE. BUT FOR A FEW WEEKS EVERY YEAR YOU TAKE A BREAK FROM THE PLATE SPINNING TO DO SOME THING ELSE. WHICH SEEMS TO ME EVEN MORE DIFFICULT. CERTAINLY MORE DANGEROUS. HOW DID THAT START? DAVID. THAT STARTED WHEN I WAS WATCHING A PROGRAMME. 1993 CHRISTMAS TIME. ABOUT SARAJEVO AND I SAW THE DEVASTATION THAT WAS HAPPENING THERE. I REALLY FELT I WANTED TO GO OUT AND HELP. SO I CONTACTED ... AID AGENCY AND WITHIN 3 OR 4 DAYS I WAS OUT IN SARAJEVO. I HAD LEFT MY FLAT IN HAMPSTEAD AND I WAS WORKING UNDER GROUND IN A HOSPITAL IN THE MIDDLE OF ... SARAJEVO. FIVE OR SIX WEEKS AND I LOVED EVERY SINGLE MINUTE OF IT. I LOVED IT BECAUSE

A LIGHT WENT ON IN MY HEAD. MY ALTRUISTIC GENE GOT TURNED ON. I THOUGHT THIS IS WHAT I WANT TO DO FOR THE REST OF MY LIFE. EDDIE WHAT INSPIRED THAT DO YOU THINK IN YOU? I CANNOT STAND TO SEE PEOPLE SUFFERING. ANYWHERE AND WHEN PEOPLE SUFFER AND THEY HAVE NOBODY TO HELP THEM...THAT'S THE ANSWER. THAT'S POWER? THE ONLY DREAM WHY I DO IT. EDDIE HAVE YOU BEEN IN THAT SORT OF SURPRISE I AM EXPRESSING TO YOU? DAVID WELL THERE IS A CORE GROUP... PEOPLE WHO HAVE BEEN DOING... MANY YEARS AND I AM PART... ONE OF THOSE GROUP OF PEOPLE. THE YOU SEE. AND KIDS NO SURPRISE AND THERE ARE A HARD CORE GROUP AND IT'S JUST THE SKY AND ONE END OF THE BELL CURVE. THE NORMALITY BELL CURVE. AND MY FEAR OF IT THAT END. YOU SEE THIS KIND OF WORK. EDDIE. THAT'S MEDECINS SANS FRONTIERES AND THE INTERNATIONAL RED CROSS DAVID YES MOST OF IT IS MÉDECINS SANS FRONTIERES. A LOT OF IT IS I.C.R.C. THIS TIME I WENT TO WORK WITH SYRIA RELIEF WHICH WAS A SYRIAN CHARITY. EDDIE THIS WAS JUST A FEW WEEKS/MONTHS AGO AND YOU WOULD. HAVE SEEN THE SYRIA ROUTE WHEN YOU HAVE SOME IDEA WHAT TO EXPECT. TELL ME WHAT IT WAS LIKE WHEN YOU GOT THERE? DAVID WELL IT WAS VERY DIFFICULT TO GET ACROSS THE BORDER. THEN WAS A LOT OF ISLAMIC FUNDEMENTALISTS. AT THE ROUTE AND THAT SCREED ME SLIGHTLY. I WORKED IN ONE OF THE MAJOR CITIES IN THE NORTH AND I DON'T WANT TO SAY WHERE. I WORKED IN HELL WHAT SECURITY ... THIS ... WORKS IN THESE HOSPITALS. FIELD HOSPITALS BECAUSE THEY WILL BE TARGETED BY WHO ARE TARGETING THE HOSPITALS... ALSO HAVE FALSE NAMES AND I HAD A FALSE NAME AS WELL AND WE USED TO CHANGE OUR NAMES EVERY 3 MONTHS. OR SO THAT NOBODY KNOWS WHO IS WHO. EXCEPT THOSE WHO ARE WORKING IN THE HOSPITALS AND SO NONE OF THEM ARE ... AND HIGH RATED WITH BANNERS ON RED CROSSES LIKE. THIS. THEY ARE ALL HIDDEN FROM VIEW. EDDIE THEY ARE SECRET HOSPITALS? DAVID THEY ARE SECRET HOSPITALS. THEY ARE SECRET BECAUSE IF THE GOVERNMENT KNEW THEY WERE THERE THEY WOULD PROBABLY TARGET THEM. EDDIE YOU HAVE BEEN IN HARM WAYS MORE WAR ZONES THAN I HAVE. WHAT HAPPEN TO THE NOTION. THAT MEDICAL PROFESSIONALS. CAN GET ON WITH THEIR JOB AND GO ABOUT THEIR BUSINESS. WELL THAT SHOULD APPLY IN WAR. EDDIE YOU WOULD THINK SO. DAVID ACROSS THE WORLD OF SOMALIA. SUDAN. SYRIA HEALTHCARE WORKERS ... TARGET REALLY AS A WEAPON OF WAR. AND... YOU CAN... YOU TO BE A DOCTOR. EDDIE WORK THAT HAS A KNOCK ON EFFECT BECAUSE THE HEALTH CARE WORKER CANNOT... THE NEXT 2 OR 2000 PEOPLE AND CERTAINLY I WAS TOLD TO BE A DOCTOR IN SYRIA AT THE MOMENT IS PROBABLY THE MOST DANGEROUS... JOB IN THE WORLD. BECAUSE DOCTORS ARE DEFINITELY TARGETED. NO DOUBT ABOUT IT. IN THE HOSPITAL WHERE I WORKED THERE WAS A GROUP OF SO 60 PEOPLE SOME OF THEM

WERE DOCTORS SOME OF THEM WERE PEOPLE WHO JUST WANTED TO HELP WAS TYPED. ONE OF THE WORST THINGS THAT HAPPENED WAS THAT I OPERATED ON SHOPKEEPERS I.T. CONSULTANTS. PEOPLE LIKE THAT DOING MEDICAL JOBS BECAUSE A LOT ON A 14 YEAR OLD BOY WHO WAS SHOT IN THE LEG AND HE HAD A CHRONIC PROBLEM WITH OF THE DOCTORS HAD LEFT AND NURSES AND LEFT AND SO THEY WERE HELPING. HIS ARTERY THAT HAD BLOWN UP HUGELY. IT'S CALLED ANEURYSM. IT IS A MASSIVE HAVE A STORY TO TELL. THEIR PARENTS ARE IN PRISON. LOTS OF THEIR RELATIVES. HAVE BEEN BLOOD VESSEL AND IF EVERYBODY. WOULD HAVE JUST KILLED. THEY FALL ASLEEP A STORY TO TELL. THEY HAVE GOT TOGETHER... THEY ARE ALL LIVING MANY ELECTED OPERATIONS. I OPERATED ON THIS YOUNG BOY AND 4 HOURS LATER AND WORKING IN THIS HOSPITAL. ANY DAY ANY MOMENT... WHO HAVE BEEN TARGETED DOWN SOME THING SERIOUS HAD HAPPENED TO HIM. HE BECAME WORSE. AND WORSE AND WORSE YOU PROBABLY DIDN'T HAVE A TYPICAL DAY FROM THE SOUND OF IT BUT CAN YOU. THE FOLLOWING DAY. AND HE HAD BEEN GIVEN THE WRONG CROSS MATCHED BLOOD. AND TELL ME WHAT WOULD HAPPEN WHEN YOU GOT INTO WORK? DAVID. I LIVED IN THE THIS WAS ONE OF THE BIGGEST UPSETS I HAD. EDDIE AND LOTS OF THE INJURIES WERE HOSPITAL. SO WE LIVED... DOWN STAIRS. UNDERGROUND WAS ... WE OPERATING FROM THE SNIPERS. YET THEY WERE CIVILIAN WOUNDS. THEY WEREN'T FIGHTERS? THEATRE. ANOTHER FLOOR ON TOP OF THAT WERE THE WARDS AND WE LIVED ON DAVID. NO. ON ANY FIGHTERS. THE INJURIES. I SAW WERE WOMEN TOP OF THERE. AND ON THE TOP OF THAT WAS A PLACE. SO WE COULD HAVE SOME WANDERING ABOUT. THEIR JOBS. HARDLY... ANY FIGHTERS IN MY TIME THERE MAYBE FOOD AND RELAX. AND EVERY DAY I WOULD TURN TO MY COLLEGE WHO WAS A I OPERATED ON ONE OR TWO FIGHTERS... MANY BUT... WERE CIVILIAN

SURGEON. A YOUNG BRILLIANT SYRIA. A BRITISH DOCTOR. WHO CAME TO LOOK EDDIE THEY WERE HIT BECAUSE THEY WERE IN THE WRONG PLACE AT THE WRONG TIME? THERE AFTER ME THROUGHOUT THE DAY. LOOK AT HIM IN THE MORNING AT SIX THIRTY. ARE DELIBERATELY TARGETED. WERE THE FIGHTERS LOOKING AT ANYWAY IN A CHILD DRINKING I AM AND WOULD BOTH ROLL OUR EYES AND THINK WHAT WHAT WOULD TODAY BRING ON THE FREE SYRIAN ARMY. THE FIGHTERS LOOKING... THEY LOSE ON. RELAPSES AND WE TODAY... EDDIE EVERY DAY WAS A DAY FULL OF UPSET OR PRESSURE... SILENT RANT. AMOUNT ON THE FREE SYRIAN ARMY THEY WERE FIGHTERS. BUT MANY PEOPLE WERE ONE DAY A... THE CASUALTIES. EACH DAY WOULD BE OVERWHELMED. AND I WOULD. SAY WELL I WONDER WHAT THE BEGUINS SIDE SO EVERY DAY. THERE WOULD BE ABOUT 40 OR 50 PEOPLE FROM ONE SIDE TO THE TODAY... WILL IT BRING? EDDIE. BUT IT WAS ALWAYS THE SAME? DAVID IT WAS ALWAYS OTHER SIDE TO GET FOOD AND RESOURCES. THEY WERE THE ONES WHO WOULD BE TARGETED. THE SAME. IT WOULD START AT ABOUT 7.30. QUARTER TO 8 WITH THE FIRST GUN THEY WERE ALL CAUGHT IN CROSS FIRE. AND THE PEOPLE WHO WOULD COME INTO THE HOSPITAL. SHOT ROUND... AND THAT PATIENT WOULD BE BROUGHT IN. THEY... SO SOME OF THEM. THE ANOTHER THING. WERE KILLED OUT RIGHT. THAN INJURED. OR IS THAT NOT THE CASE? DAVID IT. NOT THE TO OPERATE. THE PATIENT... SHOT IN THE CHEST. YOU CAN GET AWAY WITH PUTTING CASE. MOST OF THE PEOPLE. THAT WERE SHOT WERE BROUGHT TO OUR HOSPITAL BECAUSE IT WAS A CHEST DRAIN IN... A LOT OF THE TIME THEY... HUGE VELVETY SO SIGNIFICANT. A FRONT LINE HOSPITAL. AND SOME OF THEM WERE SHOT IN THE HEAD SO THEY DIED BLEEDING. THEY NEEDED TO HAVE THEIR CHEST OPENED THAT WAS THE FIRST IMMEDIATELY. SOME OF THEM WERE SHOT DIRECTLY IN THE HEART SO THEY DIED IMMEDIATELY. FIRST CASE. DURING THAT. WE WOULD... THERE WERE 4 OR 5 COMING IN. PEOPLE. WHO SHOT IN VARIOUS AREAS. ARM. LEG. NECK. CHEST. AND I THINK. IF A SNIPER. WITH AND IT WOULD. CO ON. AND ON. AND ON. AND WE WOULD. SOMETIMES WORK TO A TELESCOPE SIGHT WOULD SHOOT PEOPLE. HE WOULD. SHOOT THEM ALL IN THE HEAD. 2 OR 3 O'CLOCK IN THE MORNING. AND... I WOULD CRAWL UPSTAIRS TO BED. AND I HAD THIS BUT THEY WEREN'T. SHOT IN VARIOUS PARTS OF THEIR ANATOMY. EDDIE SIMPLY BUT FUNNY BED WHERE I WOULD SLIDE ALL OVER THE PLACE. IT WAS SLIGHTLY CONVEX. THEY WERE TRYING TO INJURE THEM. DAVID. I THINK SO. I THINK SO. EDDIE. I AM SHOCKED AND I WOULD BE SLIDING OFF THIS BED IN THIS FUNNY STATE OR STUPOR BY THAT. DAVID. YOU WELL I AM THE ONLY. WHY SHOCKED AT THE ANIMAL TO. GAUGE AND I MEANT AND I WOULD. BE DREAM. AND THEN 5 HOURS LATER. I WAS BACK DOWN IN THE OPERATING CHILDREN. THAT WERE SHOT. REALLY. I SHOCKED. THAT IT ONLY REALLY. HIT ME WHEN I CAME THEATRE. EDDIE HOW DID YOU COPE WITH THAT? DAVID. YOU JUST DO. YOU JUST BACK THAT PEOPLE COULD BE REALLY SO INHUMANE TO OTHER. PEOPLE AND WHY YOU ARE ON ADRENALINE AND EVERYONE ELSE IS TOO AND WE ARE. ALL WORKING. BUT ON EARTH WOULD A SNIPER. WANT TO INJURE A WOMAN OR A CHILD? AND THEY NOT WE. WE OBVIOUSLY. YOU CAN'T WORK CONTINUOUSLY... THAT SO SOME OF THE... AWFUL. INJURIES REALLY. REALLY AWFUL INJURIES. THEY WERE... IF WE WERE NOT THERE SURGEON. WOULD TAKE OVER AND I WOULD GO BACK TO BED. FOR A BIT. THEN I THESE PEOPLE REALLY WOULD HAVE. BEEN TO A LOT OF PLACES A LOT OF PEOPLE WOULD. JUST WOULD GET OUT OF BED WHEN EDDIE SLIDE. ABOUT THE OPERATING. SURGEON SLIDE EVEN MORE. EDDIE. WHEN THESE PEOPLE WHO YOU DON'T GO THERE. IF YOU DON'T GO THERE? ... THOUGH. I HAVE ABOUT YES. THAT'S EXACTLY. WHAT IT WAS LIKE EVERY DAY? I WOULD LOOK AT THE DONE THIS JOB FOR ABOUT 15 YEARS. I STARTED OFF IN SARAJEVO. IN KABUL. AFGHANISTAN OPERATING THEATRE. IT WAS LIKE A BLOOD BATH. THERE WAS BLOOD EVERYWHERE. THEY WENT TO KANDAHAR. IVORY COAST LIKE THIS. SIERRA LEONE. CHAD. CONGO. TWICE I HAVE BEEN TO THE YEMEN. I HAVE BEEN TO THE MIDDLE. I HAVE BEEN TO DARFUR. AND BLOOD ON THE... EDDIE. CAN YOU DESCRIBE. THAT IN GREATER QUAKES. WHAT? I WAS IN. LIBYA WHEN I... LONDON. FORCELY. WERE FIGHTING. I NEED A CHEST DETAIL? I CAN'T IMAGINE. DAVID. SO YOU WOULD GO BACK TO FRED FOR A BIT THEN I OF PLACES. NOT. EDDIE. YOU HAVE. BEEN TO A LOT OF PLACES. A LOT. OF PEOPLE WOULD. JUST SUFFER. AND WE WOULD IMPROVE OUR MORTALITY RATE AND I EVEN MORE. EDDIE. WHEN THESE SYRIA... DAVID. STILL WAS LAST WEEK? SO LAST WEEK I WAS VERY DISTRESSED. PEOPLE. AM VERY PROUD TO SAY. THAT FOR THREE WEEKS? DURING THE WERE. ALWAYS CAUGHT IN CROSS FIRE. WHOSE EVER. I HAVE SEEN. ITS BEEN DELIBERATELY GUN SHOT WOUNDS WE DIDN'T LOSE A SINGLE PATIENT IN 3 TARGETING CIVILIANS BUT THIS TIME IT IS COMPLETELY TARGETING CIVILIAN. AND I DON'T WEEKS. EDDIE CONGRATULATIONS. DAVID. THANK YOU. EDDIE UNDERSTAND WHY THE CIVILIANS ARE BEING TARGETED? BUT IN ALL THE SYRIAN WAR YOU WILL AND SHOULD BE VERY PROUD. DAVID. I AM. NOT. IT IS REALLY THE CIVILIANS. WHO ARE SUFFERING. IT'S NOT REALLY. THE FREE SYRIAN FIGHTERS ONLY PROUD TO SAY THAT BUT I AM PROUD OF THE DOCTORS WHO. OR THE REGEME FIGHTERS. THE CIVILIANS ARE. HAVING A TERRIBLE TIME WITH THE COLD WERE THERE. THEY WERE IN A TERRIBLE SITUATION AND THEY WE CAN SEE ON THE TELEVISION. I GOT SENT A PHOTO YESTERDAY WITH A CHILD WITH I THOUGHT ARE STILL IN THAT TERRIBLE SITUATION. BUT I WANTED TO IS DIFF OFF FROM AN AIRSTRIKE THAT HAPPEN? YESTERDAY. WHY IS THIS HAPPENING? IMPROVE THEIR MOOD. I WANTED TO SAY. THAT I AM HERE TO HELP THEY. WHAT REALLY GETS TO ME AND I THINK THE THING. THAT GETS TO ME THE MOST IS THAT THEM. I AM HERE TO TEACH THEM... I DIDN'T WANT TO BE THE BIG GUY WAS SO FAR. ON. A WAR BUT WOMEN THAT HARD AND MEN. I CAN'T... BE THAT AND THINGS THAT COMES IN AND DOES THE OPERATING. I WAS ON THE OPPOSITE FLYING AROUND. MY HEAD BOUNCING. BEYOND MY HEAD AND I THINK I HAD SUFFERED SIDE OF THE OPERATING TABLE. GUIDING THEM THROUGH IT. THIS IS HOW ALOT THE TIME WITH POST TRAUMATIC STRESS MORE THAN I HAD EVER SUFFERED BEFORE YOU DO IT... THIS IS HOW YOU SEE IT. THIS IS HOW YOU STOP BECAUSE WE WERE WORKING. SO HARD. SO FLAT OUT. TRYING TO SAVE AS MANY PEOPLE AS THAT BLEEDING. THIS IS WHAT YOU DO. AND REFORT GET. THERE WE POSSIBLY. WE MIGHT SHOUT IN VARIOUS AREAS. ARM. LEG. NECK. CHEST. AND I THINK I DON'T UNDERSTAND THEY HAD NEVER OPENED A CHEST BEFORE. AND BY THE END OF IT EDDIE. HOW. DO YOU COPE SOME THING. LIKE. THAT THAT. DAVID WELL. ITS DIFFICULT. THEY WERE DOING IT BY THEIR OWN. I WAS HORRIFIED. THE THERE WAS ONE PARTICULAR INCIDENT THERE. WHALE AT. I REMEMBER SO VIVIDLY. I WAS VERY DEVASTATION. ALL THE FACTORIES... THING HAD BEEN BLOWN UP. ALL AROUND. THROUGH THAT AND I SON. THERE WAS A BOY WHO HAD BEEN. SHOT IN THE CHEST IN OUR EMERGENCY THE CITY. ITSELF A LOT OF THE HOUSES HAD BEEN BLOWN UP. VARIOUS DOMAL DEPARTMENT. AND HE HAD JUST HIS LIFE. BUT HE HAD. A CHEST. ONE AS FACE AS. I WAS DEALING. WITH HOLES. BULLET HOLES AND LOTS OF THE BUILDINGS WERE LEVEL DOWN. TO THE THE OTHER CASUALTIES. I KEPT TURNING. AND LOOKING. AT THIS BOY WHO WAS. NAKED ON THE GROUND. THERE WAS A ROUND. ABOUT. NOT FAR AWAY FROM THE HOSPITAL. AND MAKE UP THE WORLD TO THE HORRORS. OF WHATS GOING ON. BUT I AM DEALLY DISAPPOINTED. THE WHOLE OF THAT AREA IS COMPLETELY FLATTENED. BUT PEOPLE ARE GOING THAT. THAT PHOTOGRAPH HAS BEEN PUBLISHED. AND NOTHING HAS CHANGED. AND I HAVE TRYING TO GET ALONG. IN THEIR WAY AND THE BUYING FOOD. AND SELLING KNOCKED. ON THE DOORS OF VARIOUS PEOPLE IN GOVERNMENT. I HAVE COME TO VARIOUS THINGS. THERE ARE LOTS OF PEOPLE AROUND. BUT IT WAS VERY VERY DANGEROUS. PEOPLE. AND I HAVE SHOUTED AT VARIOUS MEETINGS. AS RIGHT NOW... UNITED NATIONS SHOULD ENVIRONMENT TO WORK IN BECAUSE THERE. WAS ALWAYS THAT FEAR OF DANGER. EDDIE DO SOME THING. PUT. ROOTS ON THE GROUND. PROTECT PEOPLE. PROTECT WORKERS. GET CONTINUING ALL THE SIX WEEK... EDDIE... WHAT SORT OF EQUIPMENT YOU. DAVID HUMANITARIAN AID IN. I AM VERY DISCONTENTED. THAT NOTHING WILL REALLY. HAPPEN YOU DIDN'T HAVE ACT SCANNER. OR MRI SCANNER. YOU HAVE A VERY COARSE XRAY EDDIE YOU KNOW THE. DANGER? MERTS THAT ARE. BUT FORWARD? WHAT DO YOU SAY TO THEM DAVID MACHINE WHICH IS USED OCCASIONALLY. IT'S NOT USED. ALL THE TIME. BUT THE BECAUSE YOU KNOW. I AM TAKING ANY CONTROL OF THIS. WE CAN DO SOMETHING. EQUIPMENT. THAT YOU USE AND EDDIE AT ANY TIME THAT EVERY ONE. WAS EVEN. WHEN I WAS WHEN WE WERE GOING. I REMEMBER DAVID CAMERON SAYING WE SIZED SUTURES TO SEW UP ARTERIES AND VEINS. AND BIG. SUTURES TO SEW NOT GOING. TO USE MILITARY AIRSTRIKES. WE WERE GOING. TO USE. THE MILITARY. IN UP BOWELS. YOU CAN GET AWAY. REALLY BY USING A LOT OF CLINICAL ACUMEN. WE WERE GOING TO SUPPORT. HUMANITARIAN AID. AS WE HAS IT. THERE WAS BEEN NO HUMANITARIAN. YOU CAN SAVE LOTS OF PEOPLES. LIVES. WITH NOT THAT MUCH EQUIPMENT. TO BE CORRIDOR. CREATED BY. THE UNITED NATIONS. IN BOSNIA I REMEMBER THE UNHCR. TRYING HONEST. ME HAD PATIENTS WHO WERE. SANGUINATED. BLEEDING. TO DEATH. AND TO CREATE THAT SHOULD HAPPEN. AGAIN. SOMEBODY SHOULD. HAVE ABIT OF LEAD. WE HAD A LOT OF BLOOD. BECAUSE. WE HAD PEOPLE. OF THE CITY. WOULD DONATE AND EDDIE... ARE. GOING TO DO BECAUSE. THE LIBERATION IS GETTING WORSE. BLOOD. WE DID HAVE A PROBLEM WITH CROSS MATCHING. TO INSURE. THE BLOOD AND WORSE. AND WORSE... AND THEY WORSE AND THEY LEFT IT TO LONG. NOW THAT EVERYONE. IS WASHING THEIR HANDS. AND YOU KNOW. WHAT? THAT YOU HAVE BLOOD ON YOUR HANDS AS WELL. EDDIE

DAVID YES I KNOW. BUT I WAS NOT FRIGHTENED. I DON'T QUITE KNOW. WHY I'VE BEEN IN TERRIBLE SITUATIONS. BOMBED AND FIRED AT AND I HAD NEVER BEEN FRIGHTENED BEFORE I HAD PRAYED. PLEASE DON'T LET. THIS COME TO AN END. BUT I HAVE NOT BEEN SCARED. NOT. TO GO INTO AN ENVIRONMENT EVER. EDDIE. THAT IS UNUSUAL. I WOULD. SUGGEST THAT'S PERFECT. THE ONLY. DREAM I DO IT. EDDIE HAVE YOU BEEN IN THAT KIND OF SURPRISE I AM EXPRESSING TO YOU? DAVID WELL. THERE IS A CORE GROUP... PEOPLE WHO HAVE BEEN DOING... MANY YEARS AND I AM PART... ONE OF THOSE GROUP OF PEOPLE. THE

LESSER. I AM GOING TO TAKE ANY CONTROL OF THIS. WE CAN DO SOMETHING. SURELY THIS MAY CHANGE SOME. MAY THIS WAS WHEN I SAID I WOULD MET HELLO IT UP. BUT. I. IT BECAUSE AND REALLY IT WILL CHANGE. SOMETHING. EDDIE. GO FOR LIFE. SEE IF WE CAN. CHANGE SOME THING. AND AGAIN. I HAVE TRIED. AND LIE. IT. OUT. I. IT. BECAUSE. SOMETIMES. I AM SUFFERING. BADLY. AND ITS ONLY. NOW. AND AGAIN I BECAUSE SOMETIMES I. AM SUFFERING. BADLY AND ITS ONLY NOW AND AGAIN THAT. I. AM ABLE. TO TURN. TO BRIGHT. FREQUENCY TO TALK TO HIM. EVERY. DAY. I NEED HIM EVERY NOW. AND AGAIN BUT WHEN I. DO NEED. HIM HE IS CERTAINLY. THERE.

EDDIE EVERYDAY?

DAVID E EVERY DAY. EVERY SINGLE DAY WAS THE SAME

EDDIE. AND ADRENALINE GOT YOU THROUGH? DAVID I WOULD SAY SO... WAS JUST TO TRY TO SAVE ALL THESE PEOPLE AND I WANT TO TELL YOU SOMETHING ELSE. APART FROM DOING THE OPERATING AND IT. I DIDN'T. DO ALL THE OPERATING MYSELF. I TAUGHT. MY ROLE NOW... WHEN I GO TO THESE VARIOUS ENVIRONMENTS. I TO TEACH THE SURGEONS. OPERATING. DURING THE DAY. AT TEA TIME ABOUT 6. WE WOULD HAVE. SUPPER. AND THEN I WOULD GIVE A LECTURE ON MY COMPUTER BETWEEN 7 O'CLOCK IN THE EVENING UNTILL 8 O'CLOCK EVERY DAY. THEN I WOULD GIVE A DEBRIEFING ON WHICH WE COULD DO BETTER NEXT TIME AND TRY AND DO IT GENTLY. SO THAT WE COULD IMPROVE OUR MORTALITY RATE. AND I AM VERY PROUD. TO SAY THAT FOR THREE WEEKS. DURING THE TIME WHEN WE HAD BETWEEN 12. AND 14 DURING 5 A DAY GUN SHOT WOUNDS WE DIDN'T LOSE A SINGLE PATIENT IN 3 WEEKS EDDIE CONGRATULATIONS DAVID THANK YOU EDDIE YOU WILL AND SHOULD BE VERY PROUD. DAVID I AM. NOT. IT IS...

Marlene Dumas HON RA
Helena
Oil
60 × 50 cm

Chantal Joffe RA
Red Cape
Oil
274 × 183 cm

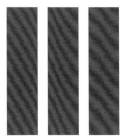

This room was hung by Hughie O'Donoghue RA, co-ordinator of this year's Summer Exhibition. His vision for this largest gallery was to focus on painting in its most elemental state, emphasising its essential constituents of colour, form and material. O'Donoghue's longstanding belief that painting remains the primary medium of visual expression is evident in the focus of his selection and the clarity of the hang. His installation enables each work to inhabit its own space but encourages dialogues between the paintings.

Kranke Kunst by Anselm Kiefer HON RA, part of his ambitious project to resuscitate history painting, can be contrasted with *Doric Night* by Sean Scully RA, a work rooted in formal abstraction and having a massive yet subtle presence on the wall. Other paintings whose emphasis is on rich and exuberant colour are afforded the opportunity to enhance one another. A discourse between works can be traced, revealing their referential complexity, as with *Looking Out to Sea* by John Walker and *Untitled* by Mimmo Paladino HON RA. A feast for the eyes, the room presents the visitor with a chance to compare the work of some of the most ambitious and influential painters of recent times, and emphasises the unique manner in which painting, particularly among the visual arts, can establish meaning.

Three memorials to Royal Academicians recently deceased – John Bellany, Maurice Cockrill and Alan Davie – are included here. All were painters of great ambition, notable artists and visionary in their work. They will be greatly missed.

Anthony Whishaw RA
Slow Appearance IV, Thameside
Acrylic
183 × 153 cm

Basil Beattie RA
Top Up
Oil and wax
213 × 195 cm

Gillian Ayres CBE RA
Tirra Lirra
Oil
102 × 123 cm

Joe Tilson RA

Stones of Venice, San Nicolò dei Mendicoli, Venusia
Acrylic
137 × 168 cm

The late Dr John Bellany CBE RA
Haunted House – Fociandora
Oil
151 × 151 cm

Dr Barbara Rae CBE RA
Refuge
Mixed media
214 × 183 cm

Sean Scully RA
Doric Night
Oil on aluminium
297 × 406 cm

Eileen Cooper RA
Spring Fever
Oil
168 × 137 cm

The late Prof Maurice Cockrill RA
Falling Water
Oil and acrylic
221 × 199 cm

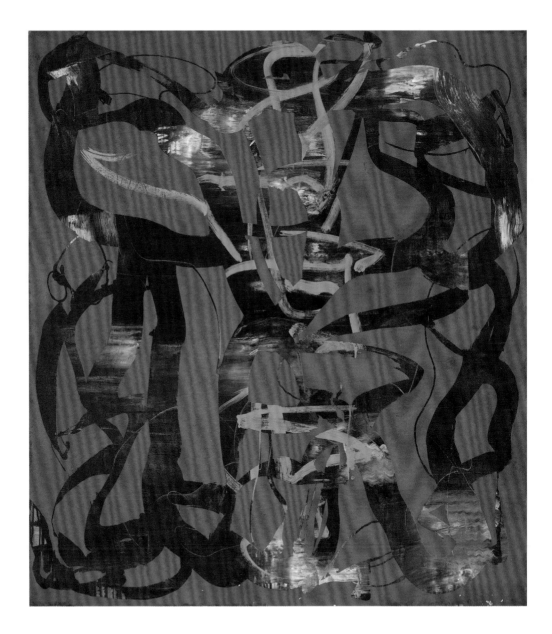

Georg Baselitz HON RA
In London Schritt für Schritt
(*In London step by step*)
Oil
304 × 184 cm

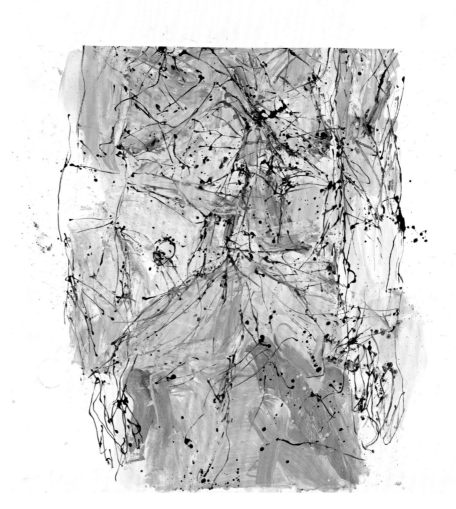

Hughie O'Donoghue RA
The Quadrilateral
Oil
244 × 234 cm

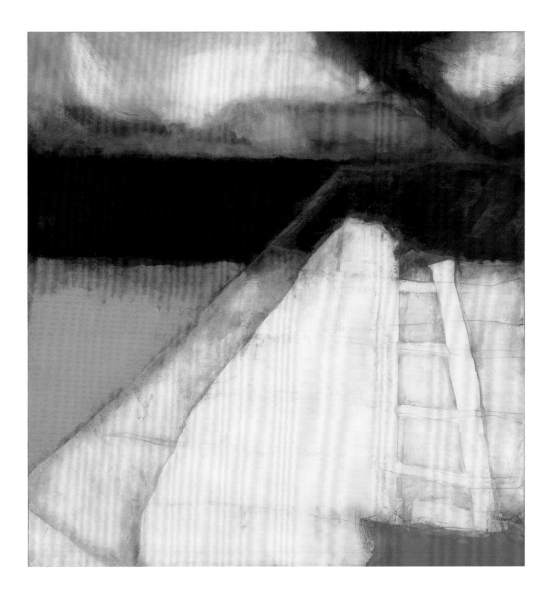

Anselm Kiefer HON RA

Kranke Kunst
Mixed media
280 × 380 cm

Christopher Le Brun PRA
Untitled
Oil
271 × 170 cm

The late Alan Davie RA
Thoughts for a Giant Bird (Diptych)
Oil
183 × 305 cm

It is immediately apparent why the print rooms of the Summer Exhibition are so popular. More than any other of the galleries, they exemplify the exhibition's democracy by presenting a rich survey of contemporary printmaking in all its forms. This year both rooms (Galleries I and II) have been hung by the artist-printmakers Prof Chris Orr MBE RA and Emma Stibbon RA. The process has been a meeting of minds, with Orr, a seasoned Summer Exhibition hanger, enjoying working in partnership with the recently elected Stibbon. Orr notes: 'By nature the process of printmaking is a very collaborative one in which the artist often works closely with others in the production of their work.' Stibbon and Orr have agreed on how best to celebrate the particular and inclusive nature of these rooms in which prints by Royal Academicians hang alongside those from the send-in, and prints by less well-known artists are positioned beside the works of those who enjoy an international reputation.

Three large, colourful and exotic images by Joe Tilson RA demonstrate his virtuosity and great experience as a printmaker; he here explores the stones of Venice, territory he has made very much his own. Nearby, Gordon Cheung's *Tulipmania 7* and *8* sound a more cautionary note. Although the tulips are delightful as floral images, their juxtaposition with pages from the *Financial Times* references one of the world's first speculative financial bubbles: the tulip craze in seventeenth-century Holland. Close inspection of these images reveals rich encrustations of paint visible on the surface, a reminder that, despite a printing process that employs up-to-the minute technology, the prints are hand-finished.

Allen Jones RA
Split Performance
Lithograph
62 × 81 cm

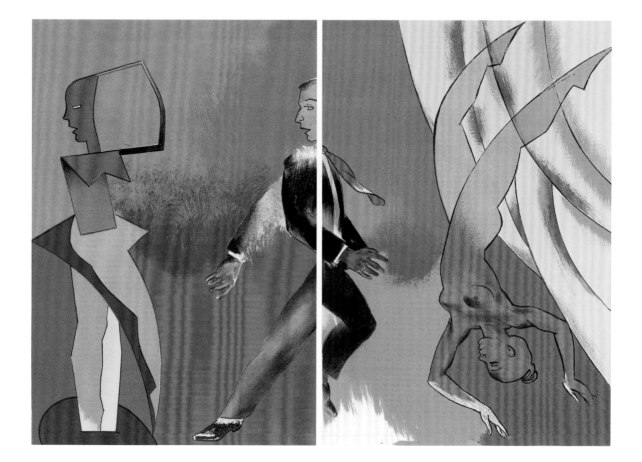

Mali Morris RA
Bridge
Screenprint
40 × 49 cm

Frea Buckler
Balance
Screenprint
30 × 30 cm

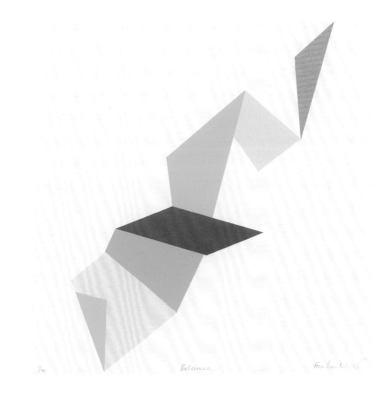

Pauline Emond
Regarde de tous tes yeux
Etching on translucent Japanese paper
56 × 50 cm

Jim Dine
British Vases
Lithograph and heliogravure with hand-work
61 × 105 cm

Eileen Cooper RA
Happy Talk
Woodcut
30 × 23 cm

Andrew Miller
The Chess Player
Woodcut
32 × 25 cm

Kevin O'Keefe
Mad Girl
Giclée print
68 × 80 cm

Ilsun Maeng
The Vixen
C-type print
40 × 60 cm

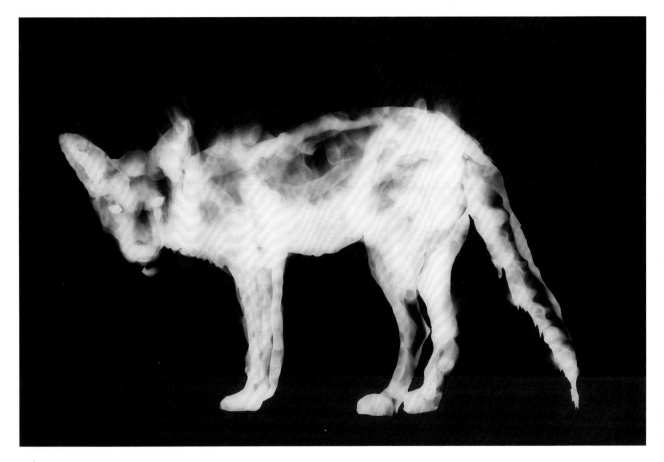

Güler Ates
The Shoreless Flower (I)
Photograph
71 × 100 cm

Michael Craig-Martin CBE RA
Spotlight: NT at 50
Screenprint
88 × 61 cm

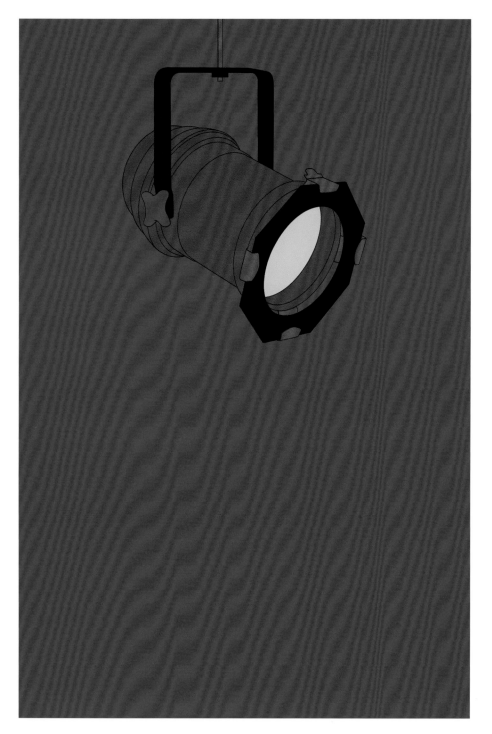

Tom Hammick
Getaway
Reduction woodcut
61 × 79 cm

Prof Chris Orr MBE RA
From the Deadwood Shed, Joshua Tree, California
Engraving
46 × 67 cm

Prof Norman Ackroyd CBE RA
Papa Stour – Shetland
Etching
16 × 27 cm

Emma Stibbon RA
Eldfell, Heimaey (White House)
Polymer gravure
48 × 52 cm

Prof Chris Orr MBE RA observes that the Summer Exhibition offers an excellent insight into emerging trends in printmaking. The use of new technologies in print production is on the increase, and the crossover with traditional methods is evidently extending the language of print, as can be seen here. The artists' books in the centre of this room are a particularly strong example of this synergy. Emma Stibbon RA is keen to emphasise the importance to collectors of prints, which are generally more affordable than unique works of art, and thus offer greater opportunities for building a wide collection.

Despite the inclusion of so many prints across both galleries and the vast range of artistic expression found here, Orr and Stibbon have managed to bring a sense of order to their unashamedly full 'salon' hang. It is interesting to determine how they have created such a harmonious result, given the particular challenges that the print rooms present. For example, the long, unframed *Ghost Sari* by Liz Rideal provides a strong central vertical on the north wall and a visual 'anchor' for the rest of the hang of that wall. The whole gallery is wonderfully well balanced, with moments of calm carefully placed to give the eye pause, such as the wonderful group of six prints by Dr Jennifer Dickson RA that evoke the tranquillity of the formal garden.

Glen Baxter

A recently discovered 'lost' Mondrian receives authentication from two leading experts in Dutch paintings prior to auction in New York

Ink and crayon

78 × 57 cm

Steven Hubbard

The Typewriter

Four-block linocut

26 × 24 cm

Magne Furuholmen
Let It Be
Woodcut
140 × 100 cm

Dame Elizabeth Blackadder DBE RA
Irises, Lilies, Tulips
Etching
37 × 42 cm

Dr Jennifer Dickson RA
The Bog Garden, Forde Abbey
Archival inkjet and watercolour print
23 × 34 cm

Martin Davidson
Chalk Cliff
Woodcut
55 × 88 cm

Lewis Chamberlain
The Winter Visitor
Pencil
65 × 109 cm

Peter Freeth RA
Would You Adam 'n' Eve It?
Aquatint
11 × 17 cm

Richard Galloway
15.35
Linocut
181 × 151 cm

Sandy Sykes
The Universe
Mixed media
115 × 90 cm

Ziggy Grudzinskas
Yum Yum
Screenprint
76 × 56 cm

Large Weston Room

Eileen Cooper RA took responsibility for hanging this gallery. She holds the position of Keeper of the Royal Academy, and as such is charged with the running of the Royal Academy's postgraduate art school, the Royal Academy Schools. Cooper is passionate about nurturing the next generation of artists and follows and supports those whom she has taught and admired in the past. Her teaching experience and current position afford her a very keen knowledge of the work of emerging artists both in the UK and abroad. She set out to ensure that the main focus of the Large Weston Room is a celebration of the work of emerging artists, but felt it important to include contributions by established artists and Royal Academicians as well, to set things in context.

Through her careful selection of works from the send-in, Cooper has achieved a comprehensive and contemporary hang containing much of interest. Trends and themes can be discerned, such as on the east wall, which is dominated by portraiture, a genre that is currently experiencing a resurgence of interest. The wide range of work on display here is notable: from a beautifully observed graphite and watercolour portrait by David Remfry MBE RA to Julia Hamilton's compelling oil painting. Cathie Pilkington's intriguing sculptures continue the focus on representation.

Prof Stephen Farthing RA
Flat Hat #3 Collie 1974–2014
Acrylic
102 × 76 cm

Paul Brandford
Mission Accomplished
Oil
122 × 102 cm

Anne Stansfield
Mediation
Oil
92 × 62 cm

http://www.ushmm.org/wic/en/media_oi.php?MediaId=4284

Paula Wajcman
Born: Kielce, Poland 1928

Paula was raised in a religious Jewish family in Kielce, a city in the southeast of Poland. Her family lived in a modern two-story apartment complex. Paula's father owned the only trucking company in the district. Her older brother, Herman, attended religious school, while Paula attended public kindergarten in the morning and religious school in the afternoon.

1933-39: Paula's school uniform was a navy blazer with a white blouse and pleated skirt. At age 9, she did the "Krakowiak" dance at school. Boys flirted with her when her overprotective brother was not around. Germany invaded Poland on September 1, 1939. Paula's father had

THE WESTON ROOMS

Anne Desmet RA
Oculus by Moonlight
Mixed media
D 35 cm

Ken Howard OBE RA
Homage to Mandela
Oil
155 × 185 cm

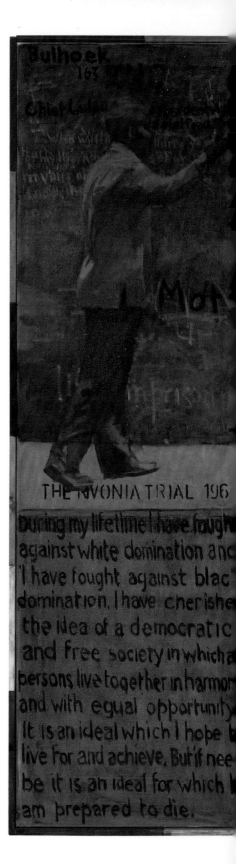

Dan Perfect
Arcology
Oil and acrylic
62 × 89 cm

Stephen Chambers RA
Gretel and Hansel (Diptych)
Oil
Each 32 × 42 cm

Small Weston Room

The Small Weston Room, the smallest of the Royal Academy's galleries, was traditionally hung in a very dense 'salon' style with only small, and often strictly figurative, works. Although in more recent years the room has been hung in a variety of innovative ways, Gus Cummins RA, who has taken charge of the space this year, was determined to undertake a full salon hang of small works once again. By including such a wide variety of styles and tones, however, he has given the room a complete makeover, giving something that was considered rather old-fashioned in the past a thoroughly contemporary appearance. Cummins's *Towards the Latter End of the World*, painted in gouache, is a wonderful demonstration of his ability to handle paint. This same sense of the texturing that paint can achieve runs strongly through the works selected here, making the hang cohesive and fascinating.

Una Stubbs
Benedict
Watercolour
16 × 12 cm

Una Stubbs
Martin
Watercolour
15 × 10 cm

Anthony Corner
Bonifazio
Mixed media
33 × 25 cm

Michael Broad
The Secret
Oil
20 × 26 cm

Gus Cummins RA
Automotion
Acrylic
55 × 75 cm

Dr David Tindle RA
Table Still-life
Tempera
38 × 30 cm

Louise Balaam
Broken Bridge, Grey Sky
Oil
44 × 44 cm

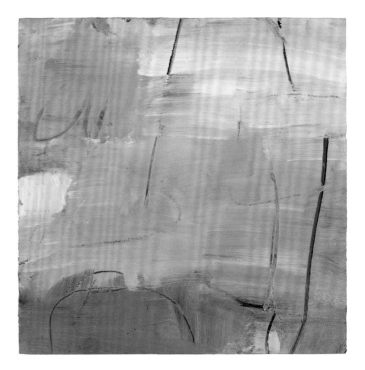

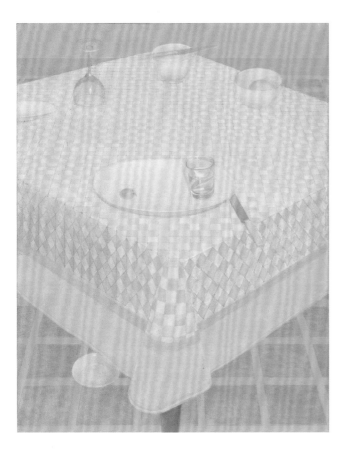

Eddie Kennedy
Mayo Elegy – Source
Oil
54 × 44 cm

David Cass
Time Pulls, Time Pools (Swiss Alps)
Gouache on wooden box lid
32 × 27 cm

Jonathan Lux
Untitled
Oil
30 × 40 cm

Aimée Terburg
Untitled
Acrylic and colour pencil
55 × 40 cm

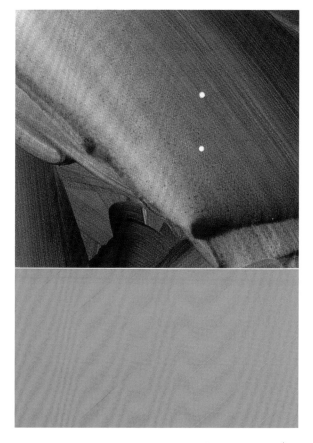

Ilona Szalay
Dream
Oil
22 × 38 cm

Robert E. Wells
The Wrong Shorts
Oil
15 × 20 cm

Tony Gunning
Kerry Humour
Acrylic
23 × 25 cm

John Miles
Samurai Saint
Mixed media
35 × 60 cm

John Renshaw
Stack
Acrylic
60 × 80 cm

Tracey Emin CBE RA
I Can't Sleep
Acrylic
25 × 30 cm

In addition to the arrangement of the larger Gallery III, Hughie O'Donoghue RA has been responsible for the hang in this room. The mood is deliberately different in both spaces, with Gallery IV pulling together sculpture and wall-based works, which has created an awareness of texture in the selection. The room focuses on the transition between painting and sculpture, examining the ways in which strict definitions between disciplines have become blurred and no longer adequately serve their purpose.

The fourth of five memorials to recently deceased Royal Academicians is sited here. Anthony Caro is represented by one remarkable work, *Elephant Palace* (see pages 96–97), executed in 1989. Made from welded bronze, the sculpture evokes classical columns and reveals Caro's interest in architecture. Behind it, and complementing its rounded forms, hangs a recent canvas by Caro's widow, the painter Sheila Girling. They met as students at the Royal Academy Schools in the early 1950s.

Frank Bowling OBE RA is a strong presence in this room, with his large, highly charged abstract paintings bursting with colour and energy. Elsewhere, the painted construction *Untitled: Foyer* by Phyllida Barlow RA flanks the entrance to Gallery V, a sculpture installation, and forms a contrast with the work of Paul Mosse, whose extraordinary constructions of humble materials – from nails to painted wooden skewers – call to mind minute organisms viewed through a microscope.

Mitra Tabrizian
Leicestershire
C-type print
122 × 155 cm

Boyd & Evans
Winter Hedge
Archival pigment transfer print
90 × 105 cm

Boyd & Evans
Spring Hedge
Archival pigment transfer print
90 × 105 cm

Paul Mosse
Nails
Mixed media
H 60 cm

Frank Bowling OBE RA
Across the Wadi
Acrylic
267 × 186 cm

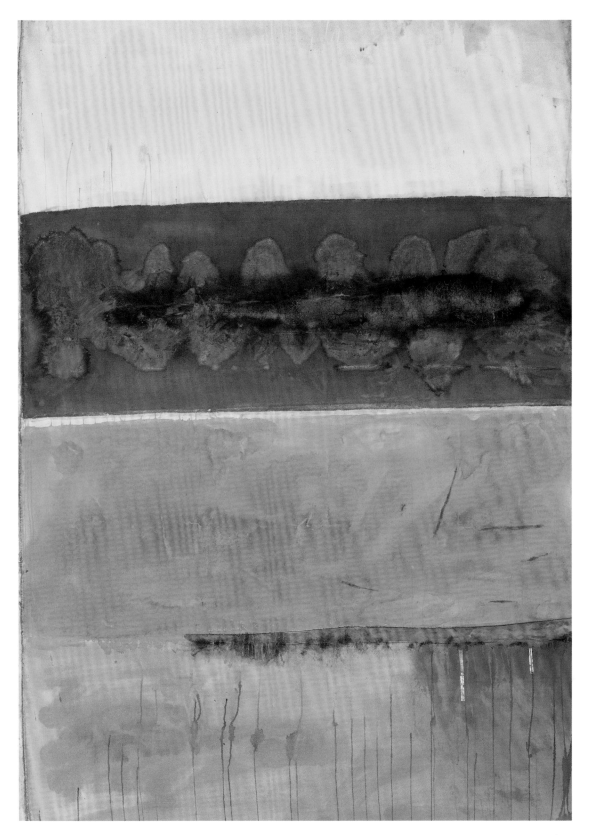

Trevor Edmands
The Wave
Oil
159 × 159 cm

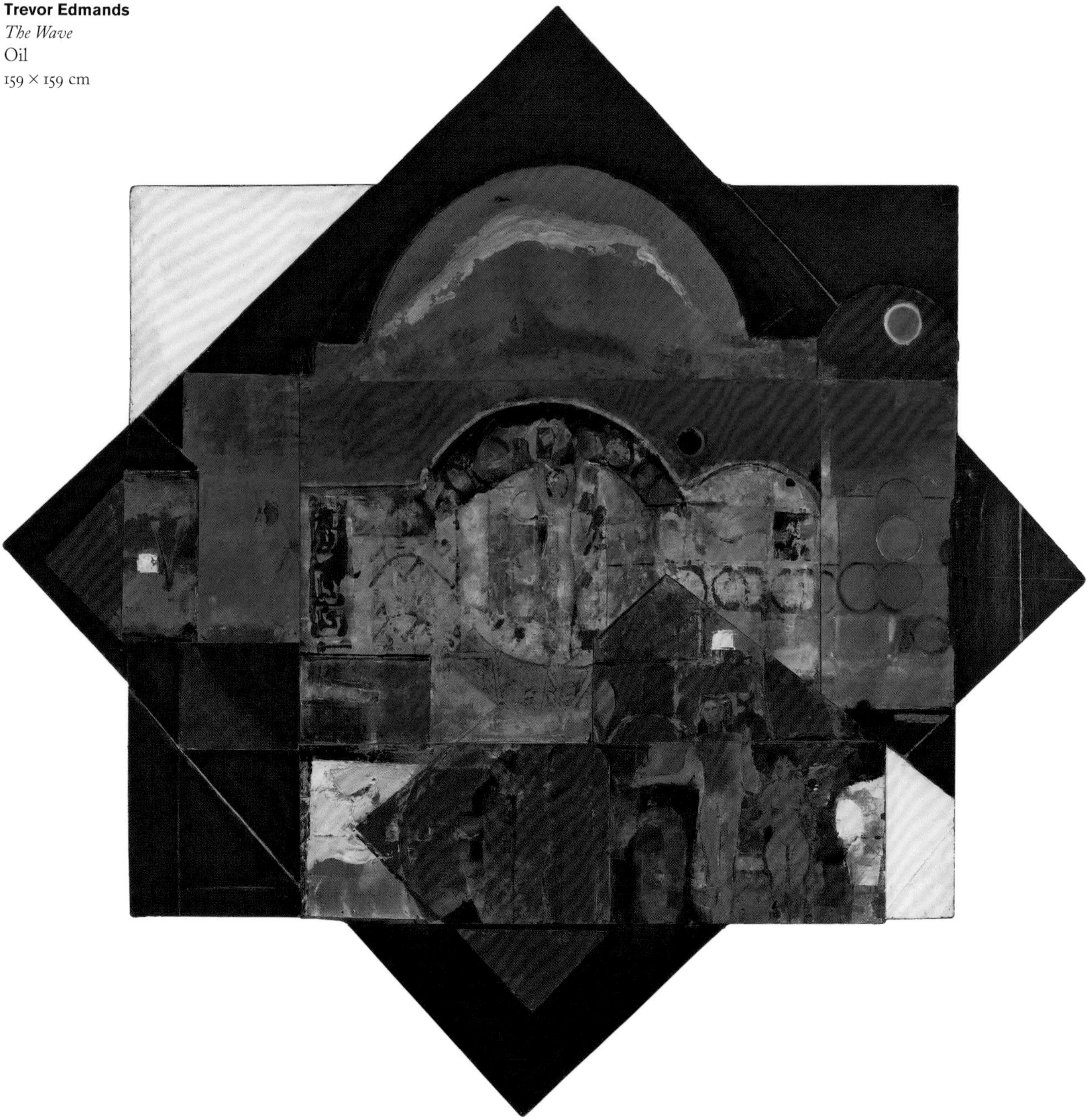

Jeffery Camp RA
Dark Encounter
Oil
36 × 36 cm

Anthony Green RA
Last Poppies of Summer
Oil
H 55 cm

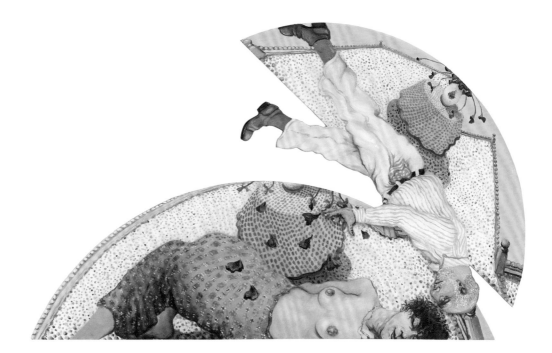

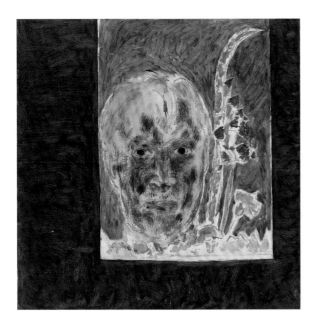

Ian Burke
Glut Ten
Oil
183 × 137 cm

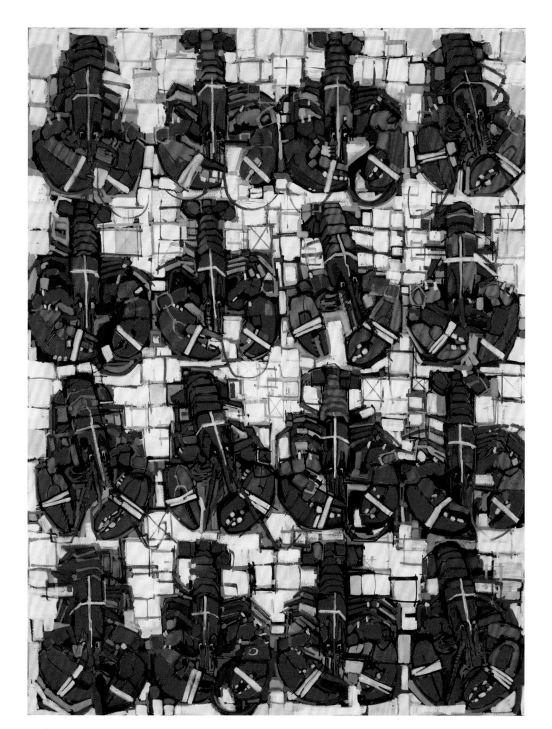

Mick Moon RA
Looking Back
Acrylic
122 × 122 cm

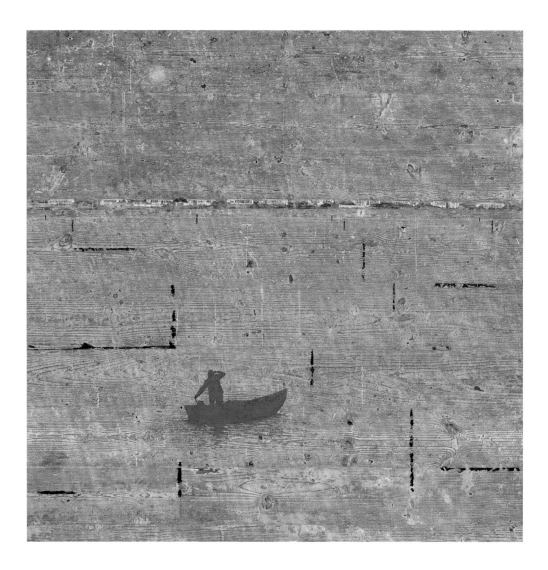

Prof Ian McKeever RA
Eagduru Study
Silver gelatin print and gouache
21 × 32 cm

Will Maclean
Portrait of a Polymath 2. On Growth and Form
Mixed media
123 × 123 cm

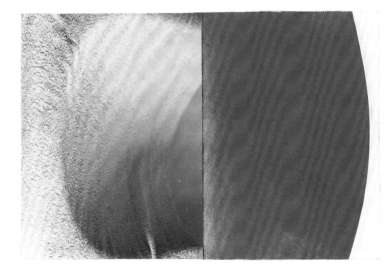

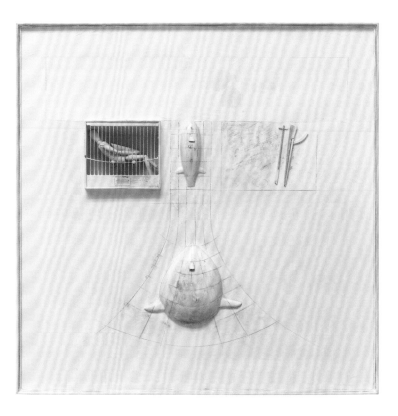

Andreea Albani
Without Title
Mixed media
200 × 200 cm

The emphasis in this gallery, which has been hung by John Maine RA, is on sculpture, with diverse elements of drawing and two-dimensional works by sculptors. Three works set the scene with their mass, materials and occupation of space. *Norway*, a substantial block of gneiss by John Maine, is firmly rooted to the ground with evidence of powerful drilling and splitting. Delicate lines are cut into the polished face. By contrast, the huge rough cube of wood by David Nash OBE RA appears to have dropped onto the floor and settled into place. Nash has scorched it to make black charcoal, which is extremely absorbent of light. Charles Hewlings uses wood in a completely different way. His ambitious iron space-frame is punctuated by blocks of timber that recall incidents seen when looking out from his window and drinking a glass of water. On closer examination we see that some blocks are carved to fit a knee or an elbow.

Beyond the spaces of Hewlings's work we are invited to explore the intimate sketches of Kenneth Draper RA and the precision of John Carter RA. Nearby, Ann Christopher RA has leant a tall prong of iron against a wall to encourage a drawn shadow. Elsewhere, Richard Long CBE RA creates a sense of distant places beyond the gallery by means of photography.

Three significant sculptures by the recently deceased Royal Academician Ralph Brown complement his powerful *Meat Porters* in the Annenberg Courtyard, all part of his memorial display, and a small but intense drawing reveals much about his working method. A larger, more recent drawing and some small maquettes by William Tucker RA extend the language of Brown's early work.

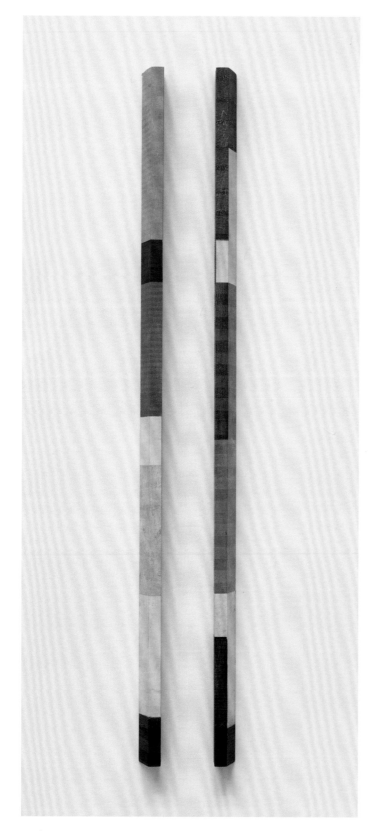

Paul Furneaux
Marking Time II (Diptych)
Mixed media
122 × 14 cm

Bill Woodrow RA
Untitled
Graphite, oil stick and
acrylic
109 × 72 cm

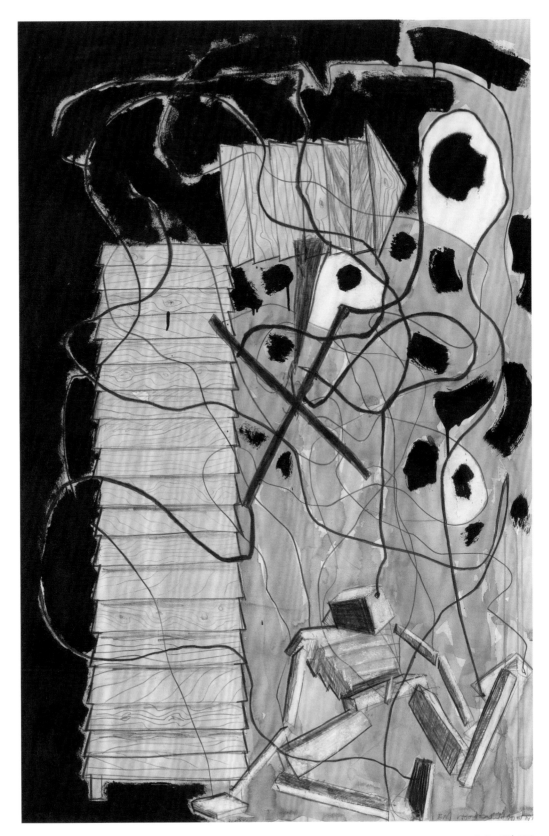

Prof Bryan Kneale RA
Little Blue
Patinated bronze
H 10 cm

Prof Michael Sandle RA
WW1 Battleship
Ink
96 × 146 cm

David Nash OBE RA
Tumble Block
Charred sequoia
H 183 cm

William Tucker RA
Study for Pomona
Bronze
H 10 cm

Prof Dhruva Mistry CBE RA
Spatial Diagram, V1 (small)
Stainless steel and epoxy paint
H 22 cm

John Carter RA
Conjoined Identical Shapes
Plywood, acrylic and marble powder
H 60 cm

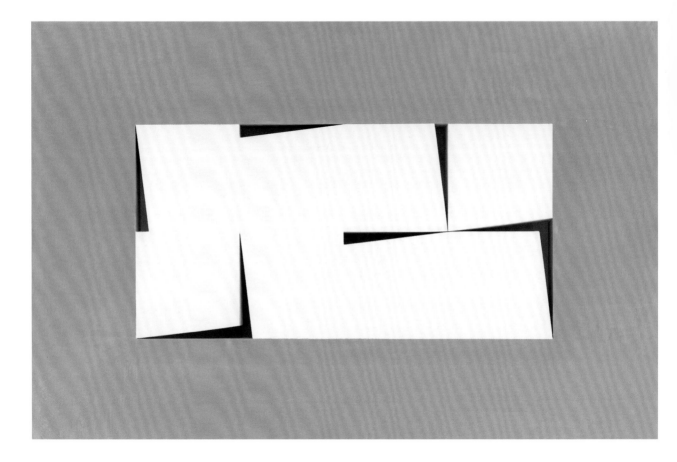

Ann Christopher RA
The Edge of Memory
Bronze
H 25 cm

Alison Wilding RA
Chimera Series #2
Acrylic, pencil and ink
28 × 38 cm

John Maine RA
Norway
Gneiss
H 155 cm

Lee Tribe
Slowly – A Lesson
Forged and welded steel, black patina and wax
14 × 23 cm

The late Ralph Brown RA
Swimming
Bronze
H 73 cm

VI

The architect Eric Parry RA hung this room after some early dialogue with Sir Richard MacCormac CBE RA. The two were keen that this year's architectural display should focus on the development of designs and the exploration of ideas during the process of conceiving and designing buildings. Parry has worked hard to avoid dominance of works illustrating completed projects.

Showing here for the first time in the Summer Exhibition is the newly elected Royal Academician Louisa Hutton of the Berlin-based practice Sauerbruch Hutton.

Parry selected the contrasting dark wall colour in this room to provide an effective setting for architectural prints and drawings. The light blue of the south wall makes a striking backdrop to the painting *The Great Northern* by the architect Prof William Alsop OBE RA.

Stanton Williams
Concept development model, office building, Moscow
Phosphor bronze patinated with antiquing fluid
H 12 cm

Sheila O'Donnell and John Tuomey
Planning model, Saw Swee Hock Student Centre, London School of Economics
Pear-wood model
H 59 cm

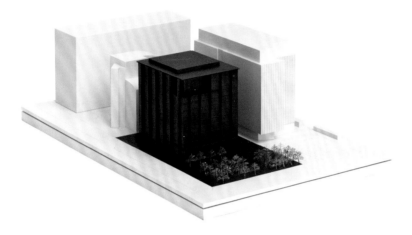

Sir David Chipperfield CBE RA
Colville Towers
Print
106 × 106 cm

Chris Wilkinson OBE RA
45/141 Bay Street, Toronto (1:700 scale)
Model
H 40 cm

Thomas Heatherwick CBE RA
Bombay Sapphire Gin Distillery at Laverstoke Mill
Model
H 43 cm

Prof William Alsop OBE RA
Wembley Car Park
Model
H 72 cm

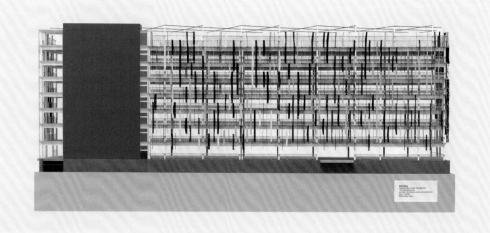

Spencer de Grey CBE RA
Norton Museum of Art, Preliminary design
Photoprint
75 × 123 cm

Eric Parry RA
A Building for King's Cross Central: Weathering Steel and Ceramic
Pencil and crayon on paper
63 × 88 cm

Paul Koralek CBE RA
Triangular Form I
Pencil
26 × 19 cm

Prof Trevor Dannatt RA
S.E.15
Pencil and collage
15 × 42 cm

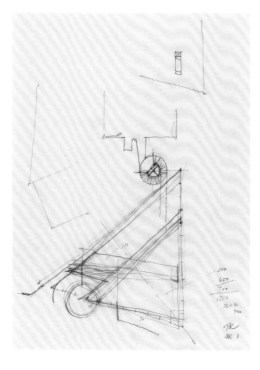

Sir Nicholas Grimshaw CBE PPRA
Collins Street Tower Studies (study models of Global Grimshaw
design proposal for 477 Collins St Building, Australia)
Model
H 36 cm

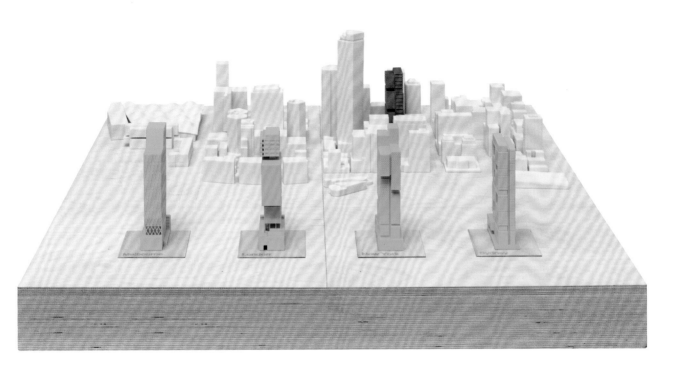

Michael Manser CBE RA

Development of the design: A Hotel in Gibraltar
Digital print
33 × 122 cm

Louisa Hutton RA **(Sauerbruch Hutton)**

Immanuel Church, Cologne
Print
68 × 61 cm

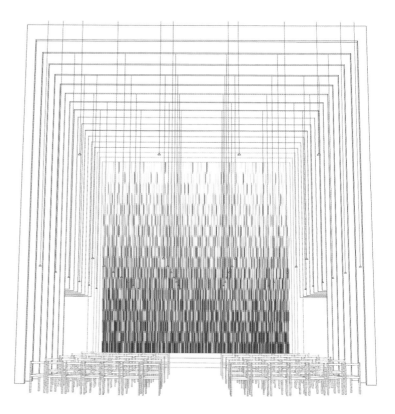

Prof Gordon Benson OBE RA
Disfunctional Family 1 (DF1)
Digital print
60 × 80 cm

Prof Ian Ritchie CBE RA
Study in Light 1
Monoprint
39 × 38 cm

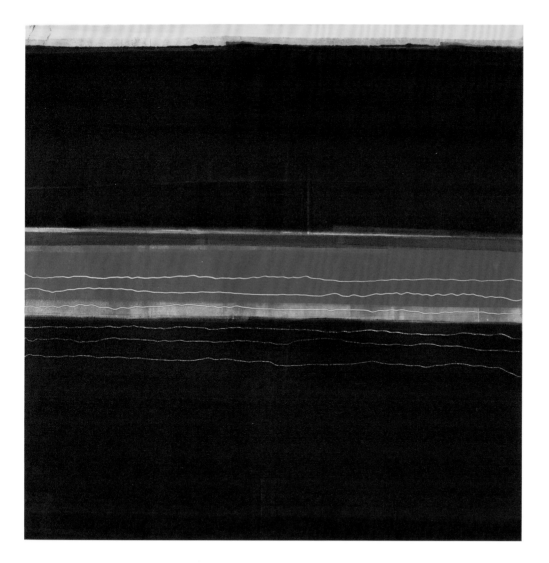

Leonard Manasseh OBE RA
Expectation
Collage, ink and paint
10 × 15 cm

Edward Cullinan CBE RA
*Design for a Visitor and Interpretation Centre for the National Fruit
Collection at Brogdale near Faversham, Kent (internal view)*
Digital print
36 × 50 cm

Witherford Watson Mann
Bankside Urban Forest
Collage
69 × 81 cm

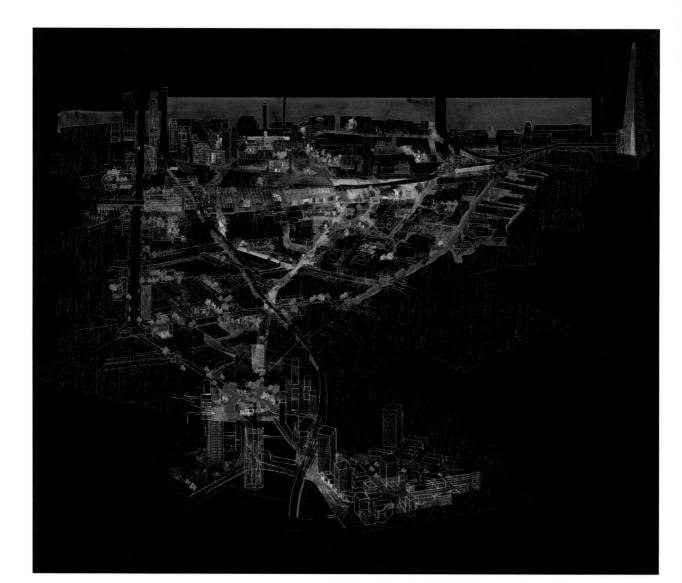

Price & Myers
Detailed construction model for the Richard Wilson RA
sculpture Slipstream, *Heathrow (1:24 scale)*
Plywood, nylon, timber
H 38 cm

Perry Kulper
Central California History Museum: Museum Archive
Mixed media
72 × 102 cm

Lord Foster of Thames Bank OM RA
Lunar Habitation, Model (1:75 scale)
CAD drawing
95 × 130 cm

Lifschutz Davidson Sandilands
Bonhams Spiral Staircase
Photograph
100 × 100 cm

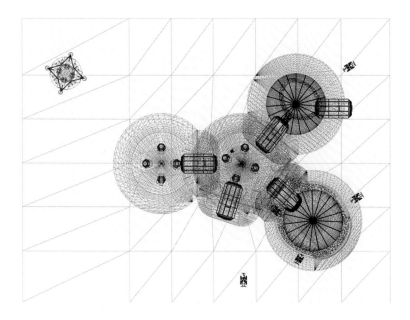

Tao DuFour
Colonnofagia
Pencil, ink and gesso
76 × 104 cm

Lord Rogers of Riverside CH RA
Berlin Forum
Model
H 15 cm

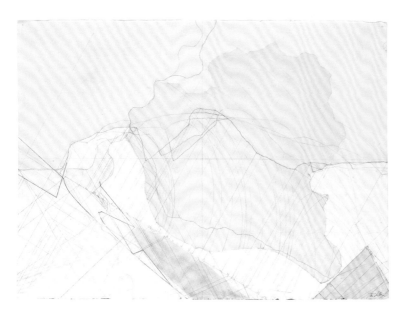

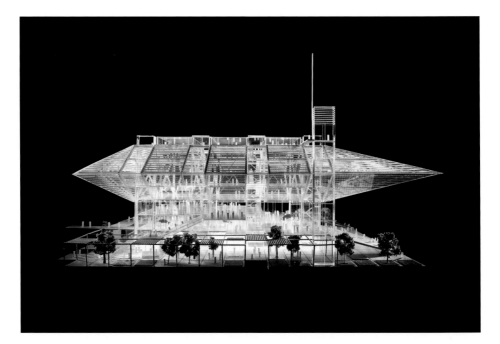

Prof Sir Peter Cook RA
Pine City View
Ink print and watercolour
50 × 69 cm

This densely hung gallery was orchestrated by Gus Cummins RA. He wanted to include so much in this room that he set himself the considerable challenge of constructing a complex grid that would not only make the works fit together physically within the space, but also set up unexpected dialogues between them. The large painting *Indian Festival on the Ganges* by Anthony Eyton RA hangs below an abstract work by C. Morey De Morand, and in Cummins's hands this unexpected pairing throws a spotlight on both. There are many such intriguing examples in this gallery.

The two large pieces of sculpture shown here continue the coming together of the figurative and the more abstract form. The large bronze figure *Free Spirit* by James Butler MBE RA squares up against *Kiosk* by Prof Ivor Abrahams RA, a work made of much less traditional painted urethane and acrylic.

Sonia Lawson RA
Assembly at Southwark, Homage
Mixed media
83 × 73 cm

Terry Setch RA
Man, Dog, Sea
Encaustic wax and oil
133 × 86 cm

David Remfry MBE RA
From 26th Street Studio
Watercolour
74 × 105 cm

Bill Jacklin RA
Crossing the Square
Oil
60 × 76 cm

Bernard Dunstan RA
Top of the Stairs
Oil
37 × 29 cm

Dr Leonard McComb RA
Farmhouse in Anglesey
Oil
46 × 56 cm

Diana Armfield RA
Bernard by the Log House, Llwynhir
Oil
24 × 32 cm

Olwyn Bowey RA
Eryngiums
Oil
87 × 81 cm

Prof Sir Quentin Blake CBE
Young and Old 11
Ink and watercolour
50 × 55 cm

Michael Rooney RA
Listening to the Aviary
Gouache and tempera
53 × 69 cm

James Butler MBE RA
Free Spirit
Bronze
H 158 cm

William Bowyer RA
Waiting for the Ferry
Oil
18 × 48 cm

Prof Ivor Abrahams RA
Sea, Sand and Shadow
Cut-out, chalk and ink
24 × 37 cm

John Wragg RA
Waiting in a Strange Place
Acrylic
121 × 98 cm

Philip Sutton RA
Tulips of Middle Summer
Oil
113 × 113 cm

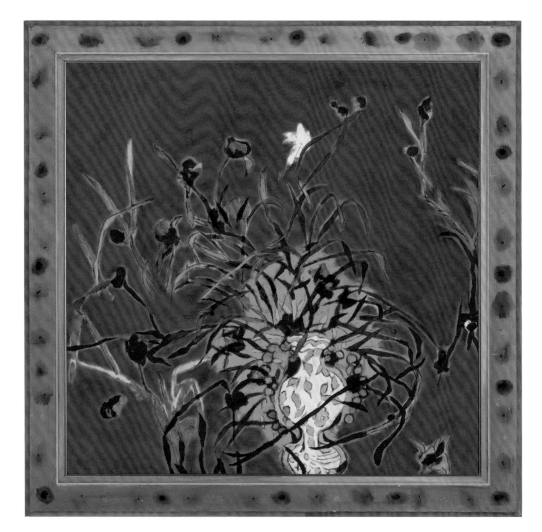

Timothy Hyman RA
Watching Over the Badger
Oil
110 × 62 cm

Frederick Cuming HON D LITT RA
Homage to La Mer, Debussy
Oil
89 × 91 cm

Anthony Eyton RA
Indian Festival on the Ganges
Oil
163 × 183 cm

VIII

The glossy *Yellow Nude No. 8 and Companion Painting* by Gary Hume RA is framed by the arched doorway leading from Gallery VII into this room, a position that certainly attracts the visitor's attention. Hughie O'Donoghue RA has repeated the circular form of Hume's companion painting and placed circular images of Marilyn Monroe and Vincent van Gogh by Prof David Mach RA, both constructed from coloured pins, on the north and east walls. A painting of coloured circles by Jennifer Durrant RA continues this theme. A series of three related drawings in acrylic and charcoal on paper by Nigel Hall RA provide a complete change of pace, hanging together on the south wall. Opposite, on the north wall, *Untitled (Lock Red)* by Michael Craig-Martin CBE RA has been hung with the long view from Gallery IX in mind.

There is a large amount of floor-based sculpture in Gallery VIII too, including *Car*, a robust piece by Stephen Cox RA. This juggernaut remains rooted here in counterpoint to the late Anthony Caro's *Elephant Palace* at the opposite end of the axis, in Gallery IV.

Prof Paul Huxley RA
Double Ellipse 2
Acrylic
152 × 152 cm

Jennifer Durrant RA
Lungo Tempo Fa – Angelos
(from the series *Ghirlanda*)
Acrylic
45 × 46 cm

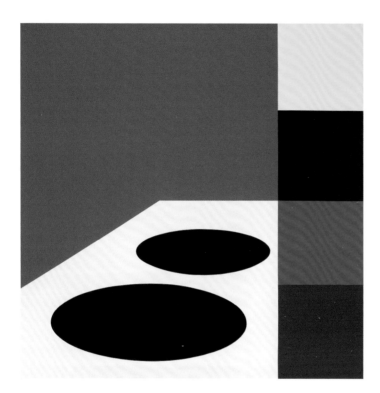

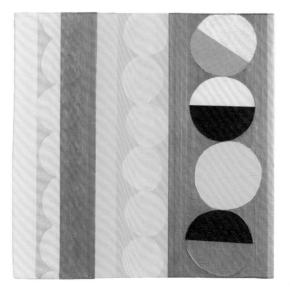

Prof Phillip King CBE PPRA
Sky-hook
Reinforced plastic and foam PVC
H 166 cm

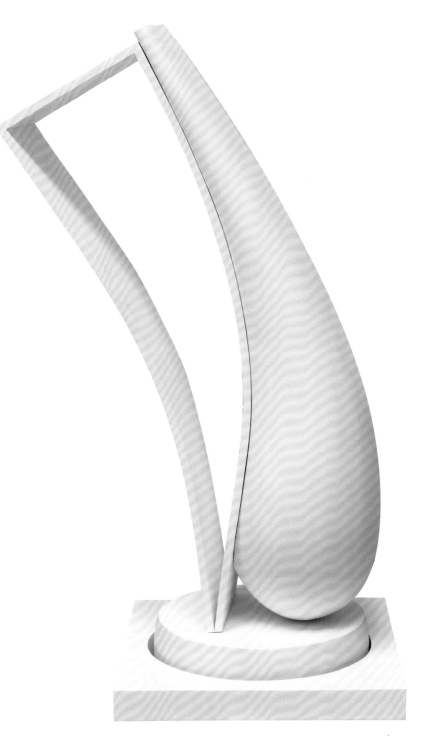

Tess Jaray RA
A Line, Light
Cut panel
120 × 72 cm

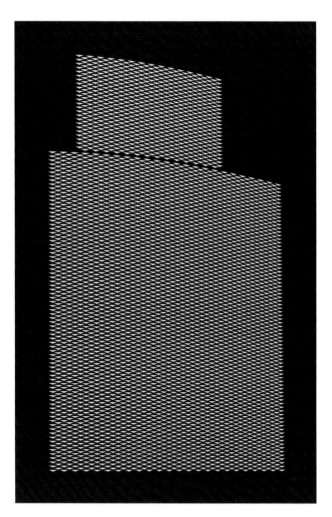

Prof Fiona Rae RA
Touch Your World, 2013
Oil and acrylic
213 × 175 cm

THE WELDON GALLERY

Tom Phillips CBE RA
Redemption
Mixed media
61 × 106 cm

Geoffrey Clarke RA
Two Troughs and a Flat Bar
Aluminium
H 154 cm

Kenneth Draper RA
Spirit of Spring
Construction
72 × 55 cm

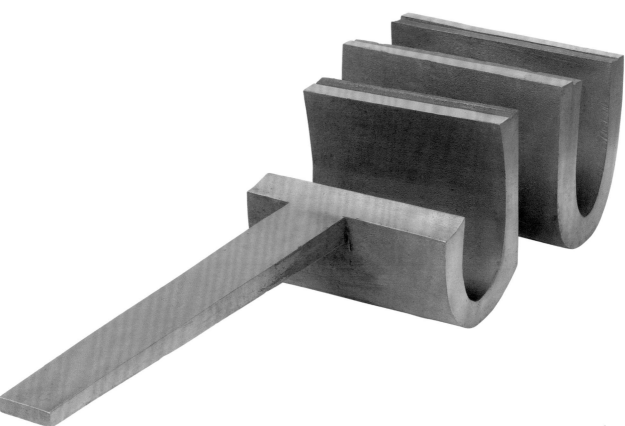

Albert Irvin OBE RA
Fortune
Acrylic
76 × 122 cm

Prof David Mach RA
Van Gogh
Pins and foam
D 113 cm

Lisa Milroy RA
Undone
Oil
115 × 115 cm

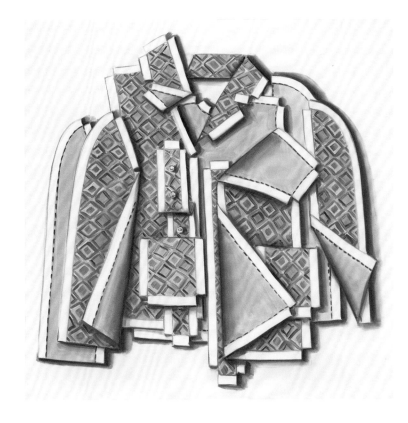

Prof Richard Wilson RA
1513: A Ship's Opera, second draft
Mixed media
134 × 120 cm

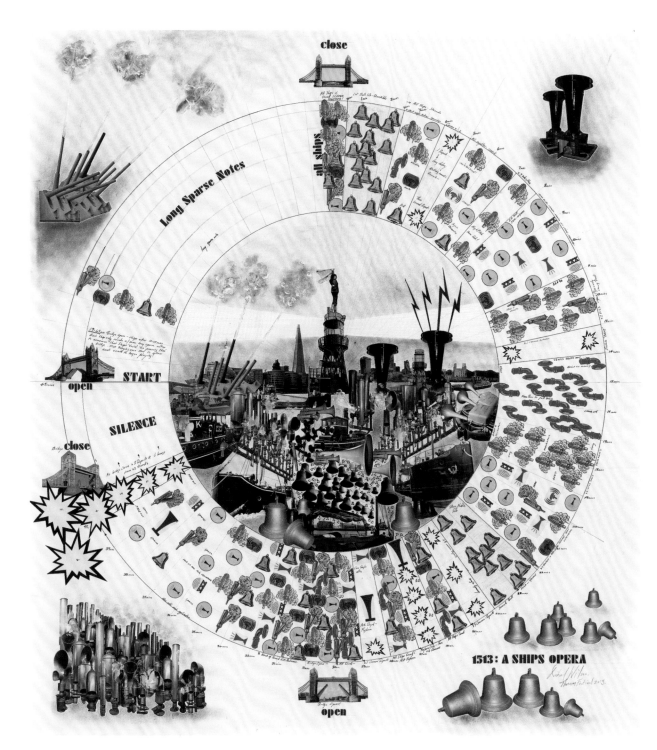

Prof Humphrey Ocean RA
Ocean Liner
Oil
100 × 128 cm

IX

The sizeable red photographic work by Wolfgang Tillmans RA on the large east wall was the first to be placed in this gallery, one of two spaces set aside this year for recently elected Royal Academicians; it can also be seen from the other, the Wohl Central Hall. Tillmans's strong colour and swirling form, when viewed from a distance, signal the end of the black-and-white theme of the Lecture Room, providing a wonderful contrast to the linear, black-and-white wall covering by Richard Woods.

Red is the dominant colour here, being picked up too in the life-size soft figure sculpture by Tim Shaw RA and the floor-based element of the new work by El Anatsui HON RA. The more muted colours of the wall-based sculpture by Neil Jeffries RA provide a contrast in tone, as does the painted bronze work by Rebecca Warren RA.

Wolfgang Tillmans RA
Greifbar 1
Inkjet print
250 × 370 cm

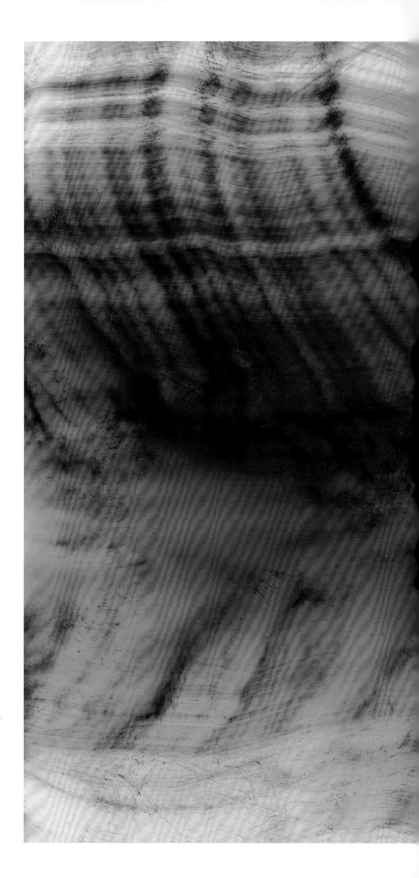

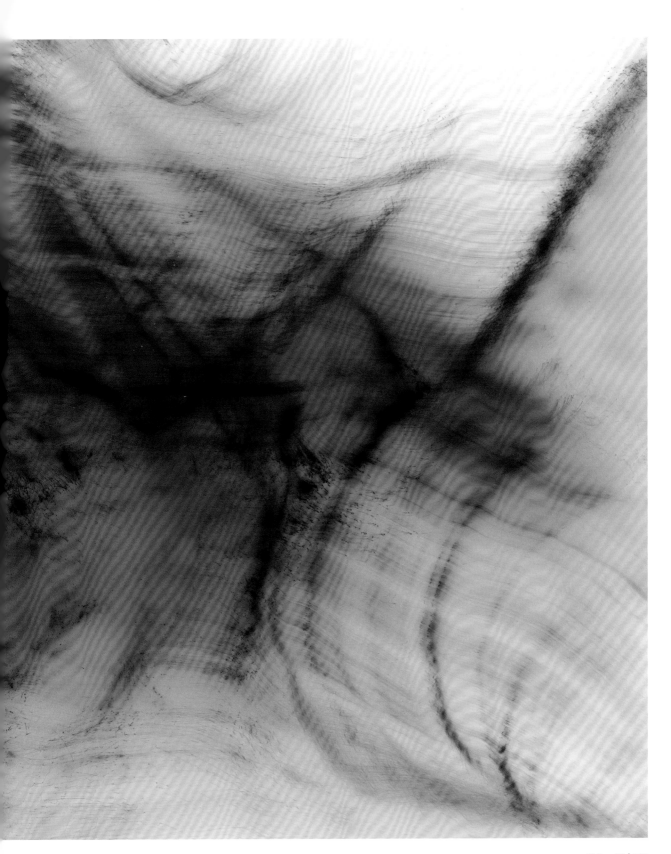

Jock McFadyen RA
From the Green Bridge
Oil
103 × 152 cm

Neil Jeffries RA
Jellyfish in Bristol Channel
Oil
H 82 cm

Rebecca Warren RA
Sieben
Hand-painted bronze
H 208 cm

Lecture Room

As a member of the Summer Exhibition Committee, Cornelia Parker OBE RA was invited to curate a gallery within this year's exhibition. She saw this as an opportunity to invite artists whose work she particularly admired to be part of the show, recognising the importance of being able to include artists who may not have exhibited at the Academy before. She has selected work by a number of fellow Royal Academicians, including Michael Craig-Martin CBE RA, Tess Jaray RA, Tacita Dean OBE RA and Richard Deacon CBE RA. Showing work for the first time in the Summer Exhibition are Mona Hatoum, Jeremy Deller, Ryan Gander, Laure Prouvost and Fiona Banner, among others.

Parker took 'Black and White' as the theme for her room. Her exploration of monochromatic tones is in part a reaction to the Summer Exhibition's usual 'riot of colour'. She says that in focusing on an absence of colour she 'hoped to create a different mood in the space, a kind of visual firebreak'.

The response from the artists was enormously positive, with all those she approached accepting with enthusiasm, and many inspired to make new work especially for the gallery, including Christian Marclay and Richard Woods, whose extraordinary wall can be seen at the end of the room.

Despite the absence of colour, the wide range of artistic expression evident here and the often deliberately humorous dialogues that Parker has subtly engineered give the Lecture Room a sense of celebratory liveliness.

Gillian Wearing OBE RA
Black and White Unite Not Fight
(from the series *Signs that Say What You Want Them to Say
and Not Signs that Say What Someone Else Wants You to Say*)
C-print type on aluminium
45 × 30 cm

Mike Perry
Shoe 2, Môr Plastig (Plastic Sea)
Digital print
50 × 43 cm

Jeff McMillan
Not Fade Away
Oil
36 × 25 cm

David Shrigley
Untitled (Spider Web Tatoo)
Ink and poster pen
42 × 34 cm

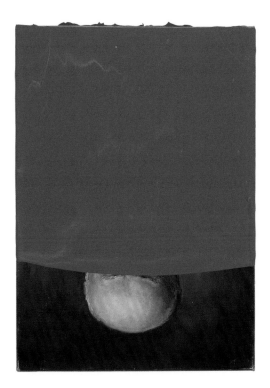

No Frills
DRAWING
CHARCOAL ON PAPER
193 X 136.5 CM

More poetry
is needed.

Richard Deacon CBE RA

4.01.11.3
Ink and pencil
24 × 32 cm

Tacita Dean RA
Still-life Roman 1–Roman 6, 2009
Fibre-based print
56 × 84 cm

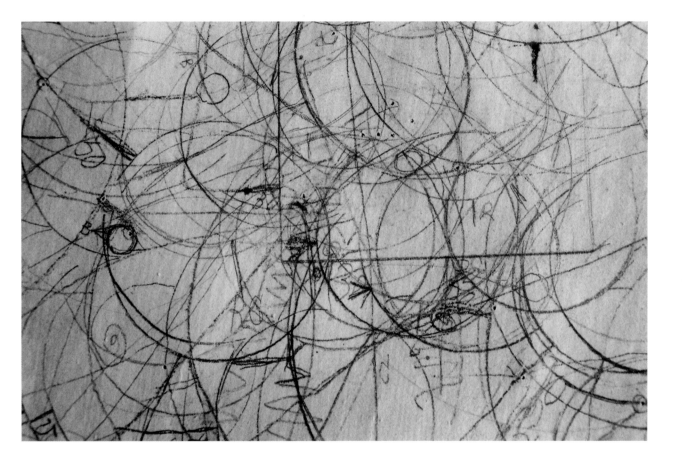

Gavin Turk
Totem
C-type print
179 × 127 cm

Rose Wylie
Black Berlin Bear's Head
Oil
183 × 336 cm

Prof Michael Landy RA
Drawings (4)
Charcoal
193 × 136.5 cm

Ed Ruscha HON RA
Wha ...
Dry pigment and acrylic
29 × 38 cm

Overleaf
Cornelia Parker OBE RA
Prison Wall Abstract (A Man Escaped) (set of 12) 2012–13
Digital-pigment prints on Hahnemühle photo rag
60 × 76 cm

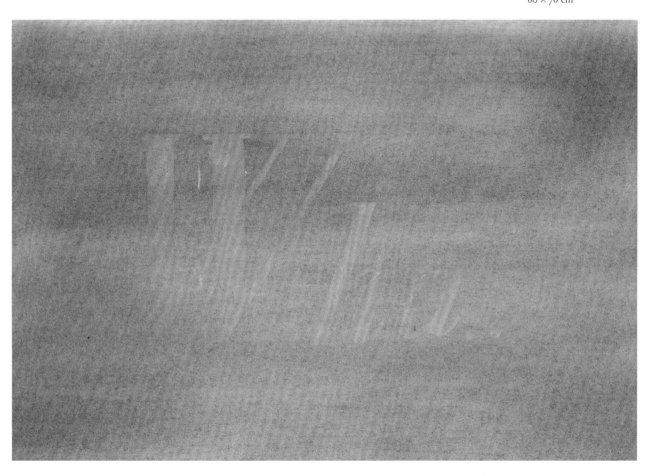

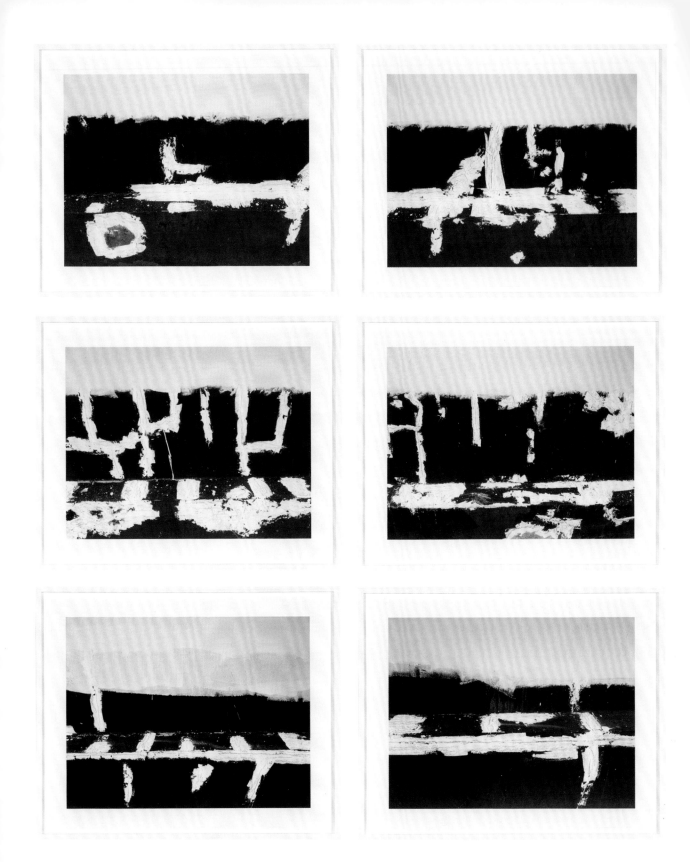

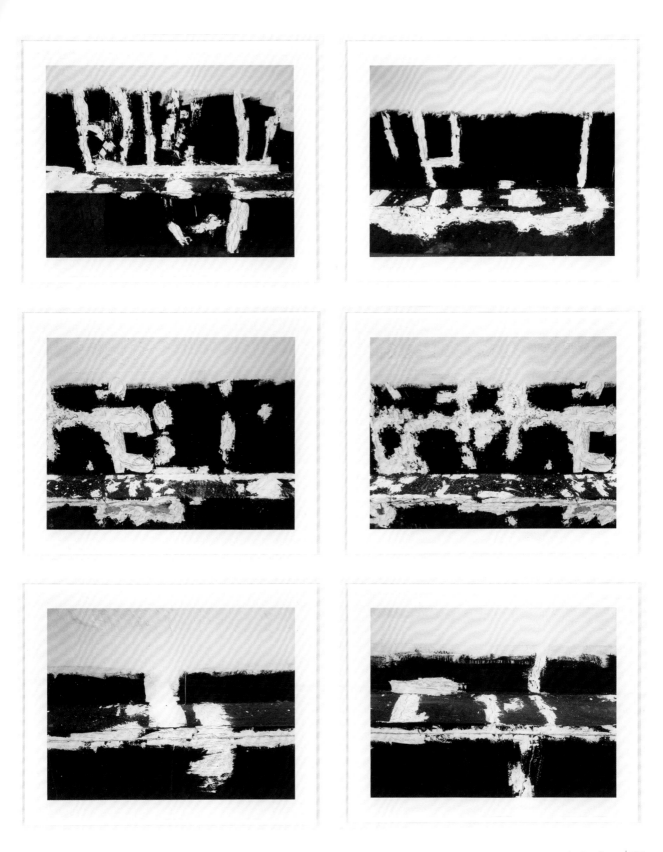

Sensing Thought, a light-based work by James Turrell HON RA, creates a tangible and physical plane of light. A room constructed within the gallery is designed to Turrell's specifications to house the work and provide a contemplative space in which to view it. The changing light source draws in viewers and holds their attention. Turrell has said of the body of work of which *Sensing Thought* is part: 'I am really interested in the qualities of one space sensing another. It is like looking at someone looking. Objectivity is gained by being once removed. As you plumb a space with vision, it is possible to "see yourself see". This seeing, this plumbing, imbues space with consciousness.'

Prof Chris Orr MBE RA and Emma Stibbon RA have overseen the selection and hang of the second part of Gallery X. Continuing the theme of light seen in *Sensing Thought* by James Turrell HON RA, the works here use lens-based documentation, digital manipulation and staged images to reflect contemporary concerns.

Index

A

Abrahams, Prof Ivor, RA **144**
Ackroyd, Prof Norman, CBE RA **52**
Albani, Andreea **103**
Alsop, Prof William, OBE RA **122**
Anatsui, El, HON RA **168–169**
Arad, Ron, RA **119**
Armfield, Diana, RA **141**
Ates, Güler **49**
Ayres, Gillian, CBE RA **26**

B

Balaam, Louise **79**
Barlow, Phyllida, RA **97**
Baselitz, Georg, HON RA **34**
Baxter, Glen **56**
Beattie, Basil, RA **25**
Bellany, Dr John, CBE RA **28**
Benson, Prof Gordon, OBE RA **127**
Blackadder, Dame Elizabeth, DBE RA **58**
Blake, Prof Sir Quentin, CBE **142**
Bowey, Olwyn, RA **141**
Bowyer, William, RA **143**
Bowling, Frank, OBE RA **9, 95**
Boyd & Evans **93**
Brandford, Paul **67**
Broad, Michael **77**
Brown, Ralph, RA **117**
Buckler, Frea **43**
Burke, Ian **100**
Butler, James, MBE RA **143**

C

Camp, Jeffery, RA **99**
Caro, Sir Anthony, OM CBE RA **97**
Carter, John, RA **114**
Cass, David **82**
Chamberlain, Lewis **60**
Chambers, Stephen, RA **65, 73**
Chipperfield, Sir David, CBE RA **121**
Christopher, Ann, RA **115**
Clarke, Geoffrey, RA **159**
Cockrill, Prof Maurice, RA **33**
Cook, Prof Sir Peter, RA **135**
Cooper, Eileen, RA **32, 46**
Corner, Anthony **77**
Cox, Stephen, RA **157**
Craig-Martin, Michael, CBE RA **50**
Cullinan, Edward, CBE RA **129**
Cuming, Frederick, HON D LITT RA **137, 148**
Cummins, Gus, RA **78**

D

Dannatt, Prof Trevor, RA **124**
Davidson, Martin **60**
Davie, Alan, RA **23, 39**
Dean, Tacita, RA **179**
De Grey, Spencer, CBE RA **123**
Deacon, Richard, CBE RA **178**
Desmet, Anne, RA **70**
Dickson, Dr Jennifer, RA **59**
Dine, Jim **41, 45**
Draper, Kenneth, RA **159**
DuFour, Tao **134**
Dumas, Marlene, HON RA **20**
Dunstan, Bernard, RA **140**
Durrant, Jennifer, RA **152**

E

Edmands, Trevor **98**
Emond, Pauline **44**
Emin, Tracey, CBE RA **89**
Eyton, Anthony, RA **149**

F

Farthing, Prof Stephen, RA **66**
Foster of Thames Bank, Lord, OM RA **132**
Freeth, Peter, RA **61**
Furneaux, Paul **106**
Furuholmen, Magne **57**

G

Galloway, Richard **62**
Green, Anthony, RA **99**
Grimshaw, Sir Nicholas, CBE PPRA **125**
Grudzinskas, Ziggy **63**
Gunning, Tony **87**

H

Hadid, Dame Zaha, DBE RA 133
Hall, Nigel, RA 91
Hammick, Tom 51
Hatoum, Mona 177
Heatherwick, Thomas, CBE RA 122
Hewlings, Charles 109
Howard, Ken, OBE RA 71
Hubbard, Steven 56
Hume, Gary, RA 156
Hutton, Louisa, RA 126
Huxley, Prof Paul, RA 152
Hyman, Timothy, RA 147

I

Irvin, Albert, OBE RA 160

J

Jacklin, Bill, RA 139
Jaray, Tess, RA 154
Jeffries, Neil, RA 171, 17
Joffe, Chantal, RA 21
Jones, Allen, RA 42

K

Kennedy, Eddie 82
Kiefer, Anselm, HON RA 12–13 36–37
King, Prof Phillip, CBE PPRA 153
Kneale, Prof Bryan, RA 110
Koralek, Paul, CBE RA 124
Kulper, Perry 131

L

Lawson, Sonia, RA 138
Landy, Prof Michael, RA 182
Le Brun, Christopher, PRA 38
Lifschutz Davidson Sandilands 132
Lux, Jonathan 83

M

Mach, Prof David, RA 161
Maclean, Will 102
Maeng, Ilsun 48
Maine, John, RA 116
Manasseh, Leonard, OBE RA 129
Manser, Michael, CBE RA 126
McComb, Dr Leonard, RA 140
McFadyen, Jock, RA 170
McKeever, Prof Ian, RA 102
McMillan, Jeff 175
Miles, John 88
Miller, Andrew 46
Milroy, Lisa, RA 161
Mistry, Prof Dhruva, CBE RA 113
Moon, Mick, RA 101
Morris, Mali, RA 43
Mosse, Paul 94

N

Nash, David, OBE RA 105, 112

O

Ocean, Prof Humphrey, RA 163
O'Donnell, Sheila and John Tuomey 120
O'Donoghue, Hughie, RA 35
O'Keefe, Kevin 47
Orr, Prof Chris, MBE RA 52

P

Parker, Cornelia, OBE RA 184–85
Parry, Eric, RA 123
Perfect, Dan 72
Perry, Mike 174
Pilkington, Cathie 68
Phillips, Tom, CBE RA 158
Price & Myers 131

R

Rae, Dr Barbara, CBE RA 29
Rae, Prof Fiona, RA 151, 155
Remfry, David, MBE RA 139
Renshaw, John 88
Ritchie, Prof Ian, CBE RA 128
Rogers of Riverside, Lord, CH RA 134
Rooney, Michael, RA 142
Ruscha, Ed, HON RA 183

S

Sandle, Prof Michael, RA 111
Scully, Sean, RA 30–31
Searight, Peter
Setch, Terry, RA 138
Shaw, Tim, RA 165
Shawcross, Conrad, RA 6
Shonibare, Yinka, MBE RA 6, 19
Shrigley, David 175
Smith, Bob and Roberta, RA 17
Stansfield, Anne 67
Stanton Williams 120
Stibbon, Emma, RA 53
Stubbs, Una 76
Sutton, Philip, RA 146
Sykes, Sandy 63
Szalay, Ilona 75, 86

T

Tabrizian, Mitra 92
Terburg, Aimée 83
Tilson, Joe, RA 27
Tillmans, Wolfgang, RA 166
Tindle, Dr David, RA 79
Tribe, Lee 117
Tucker, William, RA 96, 113
Turk, Gavin 180
Turrell, James, HON RA 187

W

Warren, Rebecca, RA 17, 171
Wearing, Gillian, OBE RA 174
Wells, Robert E., 87
Whishaw, Anthony, RA 24
Witherford Watson Mann 130
Wilding, Alison, RA 115
Wilkinson, Chris, OBE RA 121
Wilson, Prof Richard, RA 162
Woodrow, Bill, RA 107
Wragg, John, RA 145
Wylie, Rose 181

Royal Academy of Arts in London, 2014

Registered charity number 1125383

Officers

President
Christopher Le Brun PRA

Keeper
Eileen Cooper RA
Treasurer
Prof Paul Huxley RA

Secretary and Chief Executive
Dr Charles Saumarez Smith CBE

Past Presidents

Sir Philip Dowson CBE PPRA

Sir Nicholas Grimshaw CBE PPRA

Prof Phillip King CBE PPRA

Senior Academicians

Prof Ivor Abrahams
Prof Norman Ackroyd CBE
Diana Armfield
Gillian Ayres CBE
Basil Beattie
Dame Elizabeth Blackadder DBE
Olwyn Bowey
Frank Bowling OBE
William Bowyer
James Butler MBE
Jeffery Camp
Geoffrey Clarke
Robert Clatworthy
Prof Sir Peter Cook
Edward Cullinan CBE
Frederick Cuming HON DLITT

Prof Trevor Dannatt
Alan Davie
Dr Jennifer Dickson
Sir Philip Dowson CBE PPRA
Bernard Dunstan
Anthony Eyton
Lord Foster of Thames Bank OM
David Hockney OM CH
Sir Michael Hopkins CBE
Ken Howard OBE
Albert Irvin OBE
Tess Jaray
Allen Jones
Prof Phillip King CBE PPRA
Prof Bryan Kneale
Paul Koralek CBE

Sonia Lawson
Dr Leonard McComb
Leonard Manasseh OBE
Michael Manser CBE
Mick Moon
John Partridge CBE
Tom Phillips CBE
Lord Rogers of Riverside CH
Prof Michael Sandle
Terry Setch
Philip Sutton
Joe Tilson
Dr David Tindle
William Tucker
Anthony Whishaw
John Wragg

Academicians

Prof William Alsop OBE
Ron Arad
Phyllida Barlow
Prof Gordon Benson OBE
Tony Bevan
John Carter
Stephen Chambers
Sir David Chipperfield CBE
Ann Christopher
* Eileen Cooper
Stephen Cox
Prof Tony Cragg CBE
Michael Craig-Martin CBE
* Gus Cummins
Richard Deacon CBE
Tacita Dean OBE
Spencer de Grey CBE
Anne Desmet
Kenneth Draper
Jennifer Durrant
Tracey Emin CBE
Prof Stephen Farthing
Peter Freeth
Sir Antony Gormley OBE
Prof Piers Gough CBE
Anthony Green
Sir Nicholas Grimshaw CBE PPRA

Dame Zaha Hadid DBE
Nigel Hall
Thomas Heatherwick CBE
Gary Hume
Louisa Hutton
Prof Paul Huxley
Timothy Hyman
Bill Jacklin
Neil Jeffries
Eva Jiricna CBE
Chantal Joffe
Sir Anish Kapoor CBE
Prof Michael Landy
* Christopher Le Brun PRA
Richard Long CBE
* Sir Richard MacCormac CBE
Jock McFadyen
Prof David Mach
Prof Ian McKeever
* John Maine
Lisa Milroy
Prof Dhruva Mistry CBE
Mali Morris
David Nash OBE
Mike Nelson
Prof Humphrey Ocean
* Hughie O'Donoghue

* Prof Chris Orr MBE
* Cornelia Parker OBE
* Eric Parry
Grayson Perry CBE
Dr Barbara Rae CBE
Prof Fiona Rae
David Remfry MBE
Prof Ian Ritchie CBE
Michael Rooney
Jenny Saville
Sean Scully
Tim Shaw
Conrad Shawcross
Yinka Shonibare MBE
Bob and Roberta Smith
Alan Stanton
* Emma Stibbon
Wolfgang Tillmans
Rebecca Warren
Gillian Wearing OBE
Alison Wilding
Chris Wilkinson OBE
Prof Richard Wilson
Bill Woodrow

* *Hanging Committee 2014*

Honorary Academicians

Marina Abramovic
El Anatsui
Prof Tadao Ando
Georg Baselitz
Marlene Dumas
Frank O Gehry
Prof Rebecca Horn
Prof Arata Isozaki
Jasper Johns

Ellsworth Kelly
Anselm Kiefer
Per Kirkeby
Jeff Koons
Daniel Libeskind
Bruce Nauman
Mimmo Paladino
Ieoh Ming Pei
Senator Renzo Piano

Ed Ruscha
Julian Schnabel
Richard Serra
Cindy Sherman
Frank Stella
Rosemarie Trockel
James Turrell
Ai Weiwei
Peter Zumthor

190

Royal Academy of Arts

The Royal Academy of Arts has a unique position as an independent institution led by eminent artists and architects whose purpose is to promote the creation, enjoyment and appreciation of the visual arts through exhibitions, education and debate. The Royal Academy receives no annual funding via government, and is entirely reliant on self-generated income and charitable support.

You and/or your company can support the Royal Academy of Arts in a number of different ways:

- Almost £60 million has been raised for capital projects, including the Sackler Wing of Galleries. The recent phase of works includes the restoration of and improvements to the Keeper's House, Burlington House and Burlington Gardens in preparation for the Royal Academy's 250th Anniversary in 2018.
- Donations from individuals, trusts, companies and foundations also help support the Academy's internationally renowned exhibition programme, the conservation of the Collections and education projects for schools, families and people with special needs; as well as providing scholarships and bursaries for postgraduate art students in the Royal Academy Schools.
- As a company, you can invest in the Royal Academy through arts sponsorship, corporate membership and corporate entertaining, with specific opportunities that relate to your budgets and marketing or entertaining objectives.

- If you would like to preserve the Academy for future generations, please consider remembering us in your will. Your gift can be a sum of money, a specific item or a share of what is left after you have provided for your family and friends. Any gift, large or small, could help ensure that our work continues in the future.

To find out ways in which individuals can support this work, or a specific aspect of it, please contact Karin Grundy, Head of Patrons, on 020 7300 5671.

To explore ways in which companies, trusts and foundations can become involved in the work of the Academy, please contact the Project Giving Office on 020 7300 5629/5979.

For more information on remembering the Academy in your will, please contact our Legacies Manager at 020 7300 5677 or legacies@royalacademy.org.uk

Membership of the Friends

The Friends of the Royal Academy was founded in 1977 to support and promote the work of the Royal Academy. It is now one of the largest such organisations in the world, with around 90,000 members.

As a Friend you enjoy free entry to every RA exhibition and much more…

- Previews of exhibitions before they open to the public at Friends Preview Days
- Bring one adult family guest to any exhibition for free
- All-day access to the Keeper's House
- Access to a programme of Friends events

- Receive the quarterly *RA Magazine*
- Keep up to date with the Friends e-news, packed with events, news and offers
- For a limited time only, all new Friends will receive a free Grayson Perry Art Manifesto napkin

Why not join today?

- At the Friends desk in the Front Hall
- Online at www.royalacademy.org.uk/friends

- Ring 020 7300 5664 any day of the week
- E-mail friend.enquiries@royalacademy.org.uk

Head of Summer Exhibition and Curator (Contemporary Projects)
Edith Devaney

Summer Exhibition Organisers
Jemma Davey
Katherine Oliver
Paul Sirr
Jessica Smith

Royal Academy Publications
Beatrice Gullström
Alison Hissey
Elizabeth Horne
Carola Krueger
Simon Murphy
Peter Sawbridge
Nick Tite

Book design: Adam Brown_01.02
Photography: John Bodkin, DawkinsColour
Colour reproduction: DawkinsColour
Printed in Italy by Graphicom

Copyright for the illustrations is strictly
reserved for the owners by the
Summer Exhibition Illustrated.
Copyright © 2014
Royal Academy of Arts

British Library
Cataloguing-in-publication Data
A catalogue record for this book
is available in the British Library

ISBN 978-1-910350-10-2

Illustrations

Page 2: installation view of the Lecture Room. Foreground: Ceal Floyer, *Solo*; background: Omar Ba, *La Dérive*

Pages 4–5: installation view of floor-based sculpture in the Lecture Room, from left: Richard Deacon, *4.01.11.3*; Gavin Turk, *Transit Compression*

Page 6: installation view of sculpture in the Wohl Central Hall, from left: Yinka Shonibare MBE RA, *Cake Man*; Conrad Shawcross RA, *Paradigm*

Page 9: Frank Bowling OBE RA, *Across the Wadi* (detail)

Pages 12–13: Anselm Kiefer HON RA, *Kranke Kunst* (detail)

Page 19: installation view of sculpture in the Wohl Central Hall, from left: Bob and Roberta Smith RA, *Interview with David Nott by Eddie Mair*; Yinka Shonibare MBE RA, *Cake Man*

Page 23: the late Alan Davie RA, *Thoughts for a Giant Bird* (detail)

Page 41: Jim Dine, *British Vases* (detail)

Page 55: detail of Gallery I

Page 65: Stephen Chambers RA, *Gretel and Hansel* (detail)

Pages 68–69: installation view of sculpture in the Large Weston Room, from left: Cathie Pilkington, *Reclining Doll*; Tony Carter, *Reinvention of the Wheel*

Page 75: Ilona Szalay, *Dream* (detail)

Pages 80–81, 84–85: installation view of painting in the Small Weston Room

Page 91: installation view of Gallery IV featuring Nigel Hall RA, *Soglio*

Pages 96–97: installation view of Gallery IV, featuring William Tucker RA, *Chryseis*; Sir Anthony Caro OM CBE RA, *Elephant Palace*; Phyllida Barlow RA, *Untitled: Foyer*

Page 105: David Nash OBE RA, *Tumble Block* (detail)

Page 108–109: installation view of Gallery V, featuring Charles Hewlings, *Neighbours*

Page 119: installation view of Gallery VI, featuring Ron Arad RA, *Two Nuns*

Page 133: installation view of Gallery VI, featuring Dame Zaha Hadid DBE RA, *Transparent Tower Perspective*

Page 137: Frederick Cuming HON D LITT RA, *Homage to La Mer, Debussy* (detail)

Page 151: Prof Fiona Rae RA, *Touch Your World, 2013* (detail)

Page 156–157: installation view of sculpture in Gallery VIII, featuring Stephen Cox RA, *Car*; Prof Bryan Kneale RA, *Nikessen*

Page 165: Tim Shaw RA, *The Bistro Kids Gone Wrong*

Page 168–169: both works El Anatsui HON RA

Page 173: installation view of the Lecture Room

Photographic Acknowledgements

Page 6: courtesy the artist and Victoria Miro, London

Page 21: courtesy Victoria Miro, London

Page 34: photo, Jochen Littkemann, Berlin

Pages 36–37: photo, Charles Duprat/ courtesy White Cube

Page 49: © Güler Ates

Page 50: courtesy Alan Cristea Gallery

Page 130: Witherford Watson Mann Architects (Freddie Phillipson)

Page 132: © Foster + Partners

Page 134: photo, Mike Fairbrass

Pages 151 and 155: courtesy Timothy Taylor Gallery, London

Page 174: Gillian Wearing OBE RA, courtesy Maureen Paley, London; Mike Perry, courtesy the artist

Page 175: courtesy the artist and Stephen Friedman Gallery, London.

Page 179: courtesy the artist, Frith Street Gallery, London, and Marian Goodman Gallery, New York and Paris

Page 180: courtesy Murderme

Page 183: courtesy of the artist and Gagosian Gallery